Paul Hamilton Hayne

Legends and lyrics

Paul Hamilton Hayne

Legends and lyrics

ISBN/EAN: 9783743328600

Manufactured in Europe, USA, Canada, Australia, Japa

Cover: Foto ©ninafisch / pixelio.de

Manufactured and distributed by brebook publishing software (www.brebook.com)

Paul Hamilton Hayne

Legends and lyrics

LEGENDS AND LYRICS.

BY

PAUL H. HAYNE.

PHILADELPHIA:
J. B. LIPPINCOTT & CO.
1872.

Entered according to Act of Congress, in the year 1871, by

J. B. LIPPINCOTT & CO.,

In the Office of the Librarian of Congress at Washington.

DEDICATION.

TO MY WIFE.

Ah! once I held the Poet's flame
  A steadfast, heavenly star, above
The loftiest lights of mortal fame,—
And to have won the Poet's name
  I dreamed was more than love!

Now, were a Shakspeare's radiant crown
  By all the Muses borne to me,
I would not grasp that fair renown,
If thus my soul must needs disown
  Its love, dear Heart! for thee.

Even Shakspeare's fame at last shall sink,
  His titles fail, his splendors die;
But love,—*such* love as ours, I think,
Was born, o'er Time and Death to drink
  Of immortality!

So, for love's sake, but scarce for aught
  These wavering strains may sing thee, Sweet,
I bind these sheaves of rhythmic thought,
Spring-sown, but in late autumn brought,
  And laid before thy feet!

CONTENTS.

	PAGE
Daphles—(An Argive Story)	13
Renewed	32
Krishna and his Three Handmaidens	35
Under-the Pine—(To the Memory of Henry Timrod)	37
A Dream of the South Wind	40
Aëthra	42
In the Mist	43
The Bonny Brown Hand	44
A Summer Mood	46
Midnight	48
Sonnet—(Addressed to William Morris)	49
Sonnet—(November)	50
Sonnet—(Sylvan Musings—In May)	50
Sonnet—(The Cottage on the Hill)	51
Sonnet—(Poets)	52
Sonnet—(The Phantom Bells)	52
Sonnet	53
Sonnet—(The Life-Forest)	54
Sonnet—(Cloud-Fantasies)	54
Sonnet	55

CONTENTS.

	PAGE
Sonnet—(Leigh Hunt)	150
Sonnet	151
Sonnet—(Soul Advances)	151
Ode to Sleep	152
Song	155
Hopes and Memories	156
Widderin's Race	156
October	165
Here and There	167
Ode in Honor of the Bravery and Sacrifices of the Soldiers of the South	168
Sonnet—(Illegitimate)	176
Sonnet—(Vernal Pictures—Without and Within)	177
Welcome to Winter	178
Will	179
Sonnet	181
To My Mother	182

*Love and be loved! yet know love's holiest deeps
Few sound while living! when the loved one sleeps
That last, strange sleep beneath the mournful sod,
Then Memory wakes, like some remorseful god,
And all the golden past, we scarce did prize,
Subtly revives, with light of tender eyes,
That smiled their soft forgiveness on our wrongs,—
And old thoughts rise, with echoes of sweet songs,—
Soul-nightingales, in pensive twilight born,
To press their throbbing breasts against the thorn
Of sharp regret! till love so blends with pain,
And self-reproach with passion, we would fain
Re-live our years, their dim track journeying o'er,
That thus, our lost Belovèd, lost no more
In the vague distances of dreadful death,—
Might read our hearts, and feel what passionate breath
Half stifled once, is quick to thrill and burn
In the keen fervor of that love's return,
Whose kiss once dropped on heedless eyes and brow,
Is all of heaven we madly yearn for now!*

LEGENDS AND LYRICS.

DAPHLES.

AN ARGIVE STORY.

Once on the throne of Argos sat a maid,—
Daphles the fair; serene and unafraid
She ruled her realm, for the rough folk were brought
To worship one they deemed divinely wrought
In beauty and mild graciousness of heart:
Nobles and courtiers, too, espoused her part,
So that the sweet young face all thronged to see,
Glanced from her throne-room's silken canopy
(Broidered with leaves, and many a snow-white dove),
Rosily conscious of her people's love.
Only the chief of a far frontier clan,
A haughty, bold, ambitious nobleman,
By law her vassal, but self-sworn to be
From subject-tithe, and tribute boldly free,
And scorning most this weak girl-sovereign's reign,
Now from the mountain fastness to the plain
Summoned his savage legions to the fight,—
Wherein he hoped to wrench the imperial might
From Daphles, and confirm his claim thereto.
But Doracles, the insurgent chief, could know

Naught of the secret charm, the subtle stress
Of beauty wed to warm unselfishness,
Which, in her hour of trial, wrapped the Queen
Safely apart, in golden air serene
Of deep devotion, and fond faith of those
The steadfast hearts betwixt her and her foes.
The oldest courtier, schooled in state-craft guile,
Some loyal fire at her entrancing smile
Felt strangely kindled in his outworn soul;
Far more the warrior youths her soft control
Moulded to noble deeds, till all the land,
Aroused at Love's and Honor's joint command,
Bristled with steel, and rang with sounds of war.

Still rashly trusting in his fortunate star,
This arrogant thrall who fain would grasp a crown,
Backed by half-barbarous hordes, marched swiftly down
'Twixt the hill ramparts and the Western Sea.
First, blazing homesteads greet him, whence did flee
The frightened hinds through fires themselves had lit
'Mid the ripe grain, lest foes should reap of it;
Or, here and there, some groups of aged folk,
Women and men, bent down beneath the yoke
Of cruel years, and babbling idiot speech.
"Methinks," cried Doracles, "our arms will reach
The realm's unshielded heart; for lo! the breath,
The mere hot fume of rapine and of death
Which flames before our legions, like a blight
Withers this people's valor and their might."

The fifes played shriller; the wild trumpet's blast
Smote the great host, and thrilled them as it passed;

While clashing shields, and spears which caught the morn,
And splendid banners in strong hands upborne,
And pluméd helms, and steeds of matchless race,
And in the van that clear, keen, eagle face
Of Doracles, firm set on shoulders tall,
Squared like a rock, and towering o'er them all,
With all the pomp and swell of martial strife,
Woke the burnt plains and bleak defiles to life.
So phalanx after phalanx glittering filed
Firm to the front: their haughty leader smiled
To see with what a bold and buoyant air
The lowliest footman marched before him there,
Till his proud head he lifted to the sun,
And his heart leaped as at a victory won
That self-same hour, o'er which bright-hovering shone
The steadfast image of an ivory throne.

But the Queen's host, by skillful champions led,
Its powers meanwhile concentred to a head,
Lay, an embattled force, with wary eye,
Ready to ward or strike whene'er the cry
Of coming foemen on their ears should fall,
Nigh the huge towers which guard the capital.

Not long their watch: one bluff October day,
There rose a blare of trumpets far away,
And sound of thronging hoofs which muffled came,
Borne on the wind, like the dull noise of flame
Half stifled in dense woodlands; then the wings
Of the Queen's host, as each swift section flings
The imperial banner proudly fluttering out,
Spread from the royal centre. Hark! a shout,

As from those thousand hearts in one great soul
Sublimely fused, rose thunder-deep, to roll,
In wild acclaim, far down the quivering van;
And wilder still the heroic tumult ran
From front to rear, when, through her palace gate,
Daphles, in unaccustomed martial state,
A keen spear shimmering in its silver hold,
And on her brow the Argive crown of gold,
Flashed like a sunbeam on her warriors' sight.
Girt by her generals, on a neighboring height
She reined her Lybian courser, while the air
Played with the bright waves of her meteor hair,
And on her lovely April face the tide
Of varied feeling—now a jubilant pride
In those strong arms and stronger hearts below,
And now a prescient fear—did ebb and flow,
Its sensitive heaven transforming momently.
But soon the foeman's cohorts, like a sea,
With waves of steel, and foam of snow-white plumes,
Slowly emerged from out the forest glooms,
In splendid pomp and antique pageantry.
An ominous pause! And then the trumpets high
Sounded the terrible onset, and the field
Rocked as with earthquake, and the thick air reeled
With clangors fierce from echoing hill to hill.

Bloody but brief the contest! All the skill
Of Doracles against the steadfast will
Planted by love in faithful hearts that day
Frothed like an idle tide that slips away
From granite walls! His knights their furious
    blows
Discharged on what seemed statues whose repose

Was iron, or their fated coursers hurled
On spears unbent as bases of a world!
Meanwhile the whole dread scene did Daphles view
With anguished, tearless eyes. But when she knew
The victory hers, down the hill-slopes she urged
Her restless steed, where still but faintly surged
The last worn waves of tumult; there her bands
Of conquering captains she with fervent hands
And o'erfraught swelling breast did proudly greet.
Yet her pale face was touched with pity sweet
While the chained rebels passed her, worn and sore
With ghastly wounds, and shivering in their gore.
But when, untamed, uncowed, in 'midst of these,
The grand, defiant form of Doracles
Rose like a god discrowned, her wan cheeks flushed,
And through her heart a quick, hot torrent rushed
Of undefined, mysterious sympathy.
Viewing that haughty brow, that unbent knee,
"O kingly head!" she thought, "too well I know
How bitter-keen to him the signal blow
This day hath dealt! O kingly resolute eyes,
Shrining the sovran soul! 'twere surely wise
To change their glance of cold vindictive gloom
To grateful light, and make what seemed a doom
Heavy as death, the clouded path to fame,
Lordship, and honor!" Ah, but pity came
To crown admiring kindness with a flame
Of subtler life; for he, the vanquished one,
On whom that day his fate's malignant sun
Had set in storms, that night would slumber, kissed
By a fair phantom girt with golden mist,
A new-born delicate love, but dimly guessed
Even in the pure depths of the maiden breast,

Whence the sweet sylph had 'scaped her unaware.
But when the evening silence drew anear,
And round about the borders of the world
The second night since that great contest furled
Its brooding shades, the young Queen, all alone,
Paused by the dungeon floor whereon were thrown,
At listless length, the limbs of Doracles.
"How, how," she murmured, "may I best appease
His stricken pride, or touch to tender calm
His fevered honor? with what healing balm
Allay the smart wherewith his spirit groans?"
Perplexed, and yearning, on the dismal stones
Without the prison door she walked apart,
Love, doubt, and shame, all struggling in her heart,
Till the large flood of mingled love and woe
Rose to her snowy eyelids, and did flow
In soft refreshing tears like spring-tide showers;
Then, bright and blushing as the moss-rose bowers
Of dewy May, she pushed the huge grate back,
And through the dusky glooms, the shadows black
Dawned glowingly! Next for a moment she
Stood in a timid, strange uncertainty,
Changing from rosy red to deathly white;
When, as a Queen sustained by true love's right,
She spake in mild, pure, steadfastness of soul:
"I come, O Doracles, with no mean dole
Of transient pity, but to show thee how
Thy mistress would exalt the abasèd brow
Of one who knows her not!" Therewith she freed
His fettered limbs, or yet his brain could heed
Or comprehend her mercy's cordial scope:
His soul had shrunk too low for dreams of hope,
Such swift misfortunes smote him: still, when all
The Queen's fair meaning on his mind did fall.

The locked and frozen sternness of his look
Broke up, as breaks the death-cold wintry brook
Its icy spell at noonday; yet his face
Was lighted not by thankful, reverent grace,
But flashed an evil triumph where he stood
Spurning his unloosed chains. In such base mood,
One eager foot pressed on the dungeon stair,
"What terms," he asked, "O Queen, demand'st thou here?
I pledge thee faith!" Silent were Daphles' lips,
And all her gentle hopes by swift eclipse
Were darkened. With a deathly smile she signed
The chief farewell, as one who scorned to bind
Her mercy with set terms. He turned to go,
Self-centred, callous, dreaming not how low
Her heart had sunk at each cold, shallow word
With which his barren nature, faintly stirred
By ruth, or love, or pardon, dared repay
Her matchless mercy. On his unchecked way
He turned to go, when with one shuddering sob,
And deep-drawn, plaintive breath, which seemed to rob
Life of its last dear hope, the Queen sank down,
Wrapped in a death-like trance. With sullen frown,
And many a muttered oath, he raised her form,
Frail now as some pale lily by the storm
Wind-blown and beaten; for at woman's love
He could but vaguely guess, and no poor dove
Pierced by the woodman's shaft was less to him
Than this fair spirit struggling in the dim
And tortured twilight of unshared desire;
Nor could he part the pure romantic fire
Of such high passion from the lukewarm flame
That feebly burns in sordid hearts and tame,

Not of love's heat, but vacant flattery's born,
To feed his pride, yet stir the latent scorn
Of that rough manhood such hard natures know.
Waked from her trance, with wandering eyes and slow
The Queen looked round, but dimly conscious yet,
Until at last her faltering glance was set·
On Doracles, to whom—that he might see
How a soft ruth to love's intensity
Had strangely grown—she laid her deep heart bare:
Then, with a sweet but nobly queen-like air,
She said, "O Doracles, in just return
For all this love and pity, which did yearn
To lift thee fallen, and to find thee, lost,
And slowly sickening underneath the frost
Of bleak despair, I well might ask of thee
Thy heart, with all its rarest freight in fee,
Save that I feel my virgin fame and life
Must count as pure, when thou hast made me wife,
Though but a wife in state and name alone.
Behold, O chief! I proffer, too, my throne,
Not as thy freedom's sole condition given,
But that men's eyes and scornful thoughts be driven
Away from what in me may seem as ill,
If—if—perchance, thou shouldst reject me still."
At which hard word she droops her head, and sighs,
While patient tears bedew her downcast eyes.

Now, with sly semblance of a soul at ease,
Her liberal proffer crafty Doracles
Freely embraced! They passed the prison-bound,
And that same day with silver-ringing sound
Of trump and cymbal, the state heralds cried
Abroad through all the city, far and wide,

The Queen's vast pardon; whereupon her court,—
Nobles and dames,—each quaintly gorgeous sport,
Known in the old time, bold or debonair,
With feasts, and mimic strifes, and pageants rare,
Did hold in honor of their sovereign's choice;
A choice none there would question! Not a voice,
Gentle or simple, but was raised to bless,
And pray the kindly gods for happiness
And peace on both! Meanwhile the thrall made king,
Albeit a secret anger still would wring
His thankless soul, in princely fashion took
The general homage, nor by word or look
Betrayed the festering consciousness within:
So gracious seemed he, Daphles' hopes begin
To wake, and whisper fond, sweet, foolish words
Close to her heart, that flutters like a bird's
Wooed in the spring-dawn: yet, alas! alas!
For joy that dies, and dreamy hopes that pass
To nothingness! In 'midst of this, her trust,
Came a swift blow which smote her to the dust;
News that her ingrate love had basely fled,
Whither none knew. Scarce had this shaft been sped
From fate's unerring bow, than swift again
Hurtled a second steeped in poisoned pain;
For now the whole dark truth came sternly out:
Leagued with her bitterest foes, a savage rout
Of mountain robbers o'er the frontier-land,
He unto whom she proffered heart and hand,
Kingdom and crown, had bared his treacherous blade,
And of the great and just gods unafraid,
Upreared his standard 'neath the blood-red star,
And raised once more the incarnate curse of war!

So from that day all gladness left the heart
Of broken Daphles; she would muse apart
From court and friends, her once blithe footsteps slow,
Her once proud head bow'd down, and such wild woe
Couched in the clouded depths of mournful eyes
That few could mark her misery but with sighs
Deep almost as her own. At last, she wrote
(For still her soul hailed, watery and remote,
One beam of hope) a missive tender-sweet,
Charmed with such pathos, to her delicate feet
It might have lured a spirit, nigh to death,
And straight imbued with warm compassionate breath
A heart as cold as spires of Arctic ice!

Ah, futile hope! Ah, fond and vain device!
Not all the pleading eloquence of wrong,
Veiling its wounds, and golden-soft as song
Trilled by the brown Sicilian nightingales,
In dusky nooks of melancholy vales,
Could melt the granite will of Doracles.
Each tender line she sent him did but tease
And sting his obdurate temper into hate,
'As if the deep harmonious terms that wait
On truest love, were wasp-like, poisoned things:
Her timorous hints, her sweet imaginings,
Far thoughts, and dreams evanishing, but high,
Filled with the maiden dews of sanctity,
He crushed, as one might crush in maddened hours
The fairest of the sisterhood of flowers;
No further answer made he than could be
Couched in brief terms of cold discourtesy,
Holding *all* love—the noblest love on earth—
Of lesser moment than an insect's birth,

Buzzing its life out 'twixt the dawn and dark.
That letter stifled the last healthful spark
Of the Queen's flickering reason, turned her wit
To wild and errant courses, sadly lit
By wandering stars, and orbs of fantasy.
Deeming that she full soon must sink and die,
Daphles, still true to that one dominant thought
And firm affection which such ill had brought,
Summoned her learned scribes and bade them draw
After strict form and precedents of law,
Her solemn testament; whereby she gave
Her throne to Doracles, whene'er the grave
Closed o'er her broken heart and humbled head.
But now her chiefs and nobles, hard bestead
By circumstance, and dreading much lest he,
The renegade, and rebel, who did flee
From love to league with license, yet should sway
The honored Argive sceptre, on a day
Called forth to solemn council and debate
Lords, liegemen, ministers, to save the state
From threatened tyranny and upstart rule:
Thereto the wan Queen, powerless now to school
Features or mind to subjugation meet,
Came weakly tottering; in her lofty seat
She sank bewildered, listless; all could mark
Beneath her languid eyes the hollows dark,
And—save that sometimes as she slowly turned
Her wasted form, the fires of fever burned,
Death's prescient blazon, on each sunken cheek—
Her face was pallid as a cold white streak
Of wintry moonlight on Siberian snows;
Her quivering mouth and chill contracted brows

Bespoke an inward torture, while from all
The shrewd debate within that council hall
Her dim thoughts wandered vaguely, lost and dumb.
But when her pitying maidens round her come,
And gently strive on her drooped head to place
The self-same laurel garland which did grace
Her warm, white temples on that morn of strife
And woeful victory, her sick brain seemed rife
Once more with memories; in her hand she pressed
The half-dead wreath, and o'er her flowing vest
Strewed the plucked leaves those aimless fingers tore
Unwittingly; which on the marble floor,
Down fluttering, one by one, lay blurred and dead,
Like the sere hopes her withered heart had shed,
Smitten of love; for now she touched the close
Of the soul's dreary autumn, and the snows
Of winter soon would clasp her eyelids cold.
Yea, soon, too soon! for while her fingers fold
The garland loosely, and in fitful grief
She still would strip the circlet leaf by leaf,
Till now one-half the wreath is plucked and bare,
She lifts her dim eyes, hearkening, as though 'ware
Of mystic voices calling on her name;
Therewith her cheek, whence the quick fevered flame
Had quite pulsed out, with one last quiver, she
Drops on the cushioned dais passively;
For death, more kind than love, hath brought her
    peace.

Long was it ere her stricken realm could cease
To mourn for Daphles; yet her burial rites,
With all their mournful pomp, their sombre sights

Funereal, scarce were passed, when her last Will,
Despite its humbling terms which rankled still
In all men's minds, her faithful courtiers sent,
With news of that most sudden, sad event
Which made him king, to restless Doracles.
What recked he then that to its bitterest lees
A pure young soul had quaffed of misery's cup,
And after, death's? "My star," he thought, "flames up,
Fronting the heights of empire! All is well!"
Thereon, impelled by keen desire to dwell
In his new realm, with reckless haste he rode
From town to town, till now the grand abode,
The palace of the royal Argive race,
Did rise before him in its lofty place,
O'erlooking leagues of golden fields and streams,
Fair hills and shadowy vineyards, by great teams
Of laboring oxen rifled morn by morn,
Till the bared tremulous branches swung forlorn
'Gainst the red flush of autumn's sunset sky.
Housed with rich state therein, full regally
The king his sovereign life and course began,
Striving at one swift bound to reach the van
Of princely fame; his rare magnificence
Of feasts, shows, pageants, and high splendors, whence
The wondering guests all dazzled went their way,
Grew to a world-wide proverb for display
And costly lavishness. Yet *one* there was
O'er whose gray head these days of pomp did pass
Like purpling shadows o'er the faded grass:
Wit touched him not to smiles, gay music's flow
Fell powerless on his closed heart's secret woe,
While at their feasts silent he sat, and grim.
Ofttimes the king a cold glance cast on him,

As one who marred their mirthful revelry,
And in the boisterous spring-tide of their glee
Rose like a boding phantom! More and more
He felt a vague, dim trouble at the core
Of his rude nature stirred, whene'er he saw
Phorbas draw near; something akin to awe,
If not to dread, for this old man did stand
Chiefest of Daphles' mourners in her land,
As chief of her life's friends, ere that black doom
Stole from her heart its joy, her cheek its bloom.

Just where the mellowed rays of noonday light
Streamed through the curtained gloom, obscurely bright,
Which wrapped the great art-galleries richly round,
There hung, 'mid many a stately portrait, bound
In frames of costly ivory, carved and wrought,
A picture, which the king's eyes oft had sought
With anxious wonder; for day following day
Would Phorbas, mutely sorrowing, make delay
Going or coming from the council-hall
To view that muffled mystery on the wall.
Over it flowed a veil of silvery hue,
With here and there fine threds of gold shot through
The delicate woof; and whoso chanced to turn
A glance thereon, would feel his spirit burn
To pierce the jealous veil whose folds might hide
Some priceless marvel. Now, at high noontide
Of one calm autumn day, the king again
Met Phorbas—his worn features drawn with pain,
And in his eyes the sharp salt-rheum of age—
Still poring on the picture! "*Thou* a sage!"
Sneered Doracles, "yet idly bent, forsooth,
On vaporing fancies?" Then, more harsh, "The truth!

The *truth*, old man! What strong spell drags thee here?
(Some charm, methinks, 'twixt passion and despair:)
Morn after morn, forcing thine eyes to stray
O'er yon blank mystery? Prythee, Phorbas, say
What image lurks beneath that glimmering shroud?
Perchance the last king's? Well! am I less proud
And princely wise than he? Or art thou bold
To deem *me* all unworthy to behold
My brave forerunner?" Thereupon he knit
His rugged brows, the while his soul was lit
To keen, impatient wrath. With trembling hands—
But not for fear—Phorbas unloosed the bands,
Studded with diamond points, which clasped the veil
Close to its place. The startled prince grew pale,
As there, in all her fresh young grace, did shine
The face of Daphles, with a smile divine,
Into arch dimples rippling joyfully!
Some faintly-pensive memory seemed to vie
With deeper feelings, in the low, quick tone
Wherewith the king spake, whispering to his own
Half-wakened heart,—"Certes, it could not be,
That she, who owned the glorious face I see,
Bright with all brightness of a young delight,
Yet pined and withered 'neath the fatal night
Of starless grief!" To which, "Thy pardon, sire,"
The old man said, "but ere my life's low fire
Hath quite gone out, I fain would free my soul
Of that which long hath borne me care and dole;
So, sovereign lord, list to the tale I tell!"
And therewithal did Phorbas deem it well
To show how Daphles' darkened life did wane;
How love, first touched by doubt, soon changed to pain,

And, last, blank desolation, whose wild stress
Wrecked and made bare her perfect loveliness,
O'erwhelming wit with beauty. "Still," said he,
"O sire! to her last hour most tenderly
She spake of thee, her twilight reason set
On the sole thought, '*My love may love me yet;
For man's love comes with knowledge, so I deem,
Slow-hearted man's!*' Ah, heaven! she could not dream,
But *thy* name filled her dreams. When madness stole
Like a dread mist about her, and her soul,
Wound in its viewless cerement-folds accursed——"
"Madness!" the king cried in a sharp outburst
Of wild amazement: "madness! *I* have known
The mad impatience of a will o'ergrown,
When sternly thwarted in its fiery zeal,
But dreamed not how these fairy creatures feel,
These soft, frail-natured women, if, perchance,
Love turn on them a cold or lukewarm glance
Of brief denial!" Then the impatient red,
In a swift flood,—but not of anger,—spread
O'er the king's face; convulsed it seemed, and stern.
But when from garrulous Phorbas he did learn
How the Queen's laurel wreath half bare became,
The hot blood ebbed, and o'er its waning flame
Coursed the first tear his warrior-soul had shed.
Nor could he rouse again the lustihead
Of ruder thoughts, but, thickly muttering, laid
On the fair portrait of the sovereign maid
A reverent hand; from 'midst the painted dome
Of the great gallery forth he bore it home
Unto the secret chamber of his rest;
There next his couch he placed the beauteous guest;

There feasted on its sweetness; and since naught
Of public import now did claim his thought,
No fierce war threatened, no shrewd treaties pressed,
Strangely the picture mastered him; it grew,
As days, then weeks, and seasons, o'er him flew,
A part, an inmost essence of all life,
Which touched to joy or thrilled to shuddering strife
The soul's deep-seated issues: yet, at last,
Stronger the fierce strife waxed; the bliss was passed;
And, wheresoe'er the king went, night or day,
One haunting phantom barred his doomèd way!

But ere he reached the worst wild stage of woe,
Through many a change of passion, swift or slow,
The king passed downward, nearing treacherous death;
And thus it happed, our old-world legend saith:

The more he gazed on Daphles' blooming face,
All flushed with happy youth and Hebe grace,
The more her marvelous image seemed alive;
He saw, or dreamed he saw, the warm blood strive,
In ruddier tide, with conscious hues to dye
Her lovely brow and swanlike neck, or vie
With Syrian roses on her cheeks of flame;
The more he gazed, the more her lips became
Instinct with timorous motion, till a sigh,
New-born of honeyed love unwittingly,
Seemed hovering like a murmurous fairy-bee
About their rich, half-parted comeliness:
What slight breath softly stirs the truant tress,
Which like a waif of sunset light did rest
In wandering golden lustre on her breast?

And what dear thought her bosom graciously
Heaves into gentle billows, like a sea
Moon-kissed, and whispering? Thus the king would
    task
Long hours with doting questions, when the mask
Of dull state forms and ceremonial play
With wearied brain and hand was cast away,
And he a dead maid's crafty image turned
To breathing life, and blissful love that burned
From her wild pulses and fond heart to his,
And on her mouth he pressed a bridegroom kiss.

Then the sweet spell was broken; conscience spoke,
And in her burning depths pale memory woke.
Even in that gentle shape his cold self-will
Had strangely turned, and wrought him direful ill;
Distempered, moody, sometimes nigh distraught
With ceaseless pressure of one harrowing thought,
He grew, and hapless thrills of lonely pain;
Her picture, imaged on his heart and brain,
Ruled all his tides of being, as the moon
Draws changeful seas; now in a clear high noon
Of memories bitter-sweet his soul would swim,
Anon to sink in turbulent gulfs and dim
Of wild regret, or as the dead to lie
Locked in a mute, life-withering lethargy.
Creator sweet of all his fortunes high,
Oh, that in Hades she could hear his cry
Remorseful, and come back in pitying guise
To ease his grief and calm his tortured sighs!
A thousand, thousand times this wild desire
Would wake, and surge through all his veins like fire;

Followed, alas, too soon, by such deep sense
Of powerless will, and mortal impotence,
As in red hurry up from soul to cheeks
Runs rioting, and ever harshly seeks
To drag them into gaunt, gray lines of care!
Months sped eventless, with his dark despair
Grown darker; till, one sad November morn,
Set to the rhythmic wail of winds forlorn,
They found, just where the morning's shadowy gloom
Had gathered deepest in the prince's room,
His prostrate body, cold, and turned in part
Upwards,—the blade's hilt glittering o'er his heart,
Where his own mad right arm had sent it home.
Beneath him, in soft-tinted, fadeless bloom,
Beneath him smiled the portrait he had torn
Madly from off the wall, his wan face borne
Next the clear brightness of that lifelike one
For whose fair sake he lay, at last, undone;
But whose glad smile, could *she* have lived that hour,
Had waned and withered inward, like a flower
The storm-wind blights, at stern revenge, like this,
Of love's cold scorn and passion's unpaid kiss.

RENEWED.

Welcome, rippling sunshine!
    Welcome, joyous air!
Like a demon shadow
    Flies the gaunt despair!
Heaven, through heights of happy calm,
    Its heart of hearts uncloses,
To win earth's answering love in balm,
    Her blushing thanks—in roses!

Voices from the pine-grove,
    Where the pheasant's drumming,
Voices from the ferny hills
    Alive with insect humming;
Voices low and sweet
    From the far-off stream,
Where two rivulets meet
    With the murmur of a dream;
Voices loud and free
From every bush and tree,
Of sportive forest bards outpouring songs of gladness;
    But over them still
    With its passionate trill,
The mock-bird's jocund madness!

Deep down the swampy brake
Even the poison-snake,

RENEWED.

  Uncoiled, and basking in the noontide splendor,
  May feel, perchance, on this auspicious day
    (All dark clouds rolled away),
    Thorough his stagnant blood,
    Warmed by the sunlight flood,
    A faint, far sense,
    Coming he knows not whence,
    Of dim intelligence,—
The thinnest conscious thrill that human is, and tender!

    Look! where on luminous wing
    The ether's stately king,
  The lone sea-eagle, circling proud and slow,
  Towers in the sapphire glow;
    From out whose dazzling beam,
    His resonant scream,
  Heard even here,—a note of fierce desire,—
  Hushes to silent awe the sylvan choir,
  Till bird and note in airy deeps updrawn
  Are melting toward the dawn!

    And hear! O! hear!
    No longer wildly terrible and drear,
  But as if merry pulses timed their beating,
    The frolic sea-waves near,
  Dancing along like happy maidens playing
  When blithe love goes "a-Maying,"
  And wreaking on the shore their panting blisses
    In coy, impulsive kisses;
Whilst he—poor Dullard—cannot catch nor hold them,
Nor in his massive, earthen arms enfold them,
The laughing virgin waves, so archly, swiftly fleeting!

This subtle atmosphere,
So magically clear,
Melts, as it were, upon my eager lip;
From some invisible goblet of delight
Idly I sip and sip
A wine so warm and golden
(From some enchanted bin the wine was stolen),
A wine so sweet and rare,
Methinks a nobler birth
Illuminates the earth,
And in my heart I hear a fairy singing;
Yet well I know 'tis but my soul renew'd,
Reborn and bright,
From grief and grief's malignant solitude!
Yet well I know, Joy is the Ganymede,
Who in my yearning need,
Turns to a cordial rich the balmy air;
And 'tis but Hope's, divinest Hope's return,
Which makes my inmost spirit throb and burn,
And Hope's triumphant song,
So sweet and strong,
That all creation seems with that weird music ringing!

KRISHNA AND HIS THREE HANDMAIDENS.

AND where he sat beneath the mystic stars,
Nigh the twin founts of Immortality,
That feed fair channels of the Stream of Trance,—
To Krishna once his three handmaidens came,
Asking a boon: "O king! O lord!" they said,
"Test thou thy servants' wisdom; long in dreams,
Born of the waters of thy Stream of Trance,
Have we, thy fond handmaidens, wandered free,
And lapped in airiest wreaths of fantasy;
Now would we, viewless, bearing each some gift
From thee, our father, seek the world of man,
The world of man, and pain, which whoso leaves
Better or brighter, for thy gift bestowed
Most worthily, shall claim thy just reward,
The Crown of Wisdom!" Krishna heard, and gave
To each one tiny drop of diamond dew,
Drawn from the founts that feed the Stream of Trance,
Wherewith, on waftage of miraculous winds,
Breathing full south, they sought the world of man,
The world of man and pain that shrank in drought,
Palsied and withered, like an old man's face
Death-smitten.

And the first handmaiden saw
A monarch's fountain sparkling in the waste,
Glowing and fresh, though all the land was sick,
Gasping for rain, and famished thousands died:

"O brave," she said, "O beautiful bright waves!
Like calls to like;" and so her dewdrop glanced,
And glittered downward as a fairy star
Loosed from a tress of Cassiopeia's hair,
Down to the glorious fountain of the king.

Over the passionless bosom of the sea,
The Indian Sea, cerulean, crystal-clear,
And calm, the second handmaid, hovering, viewed—
Far through the tangled sea-weed and cool tides
Pulsing 'twixt coral branches—the wide lips
Of purpling shells that yearned to clasp a pearl:
So where the oyster, blindly reared, *awaits
Its priceless soul*—she lets the dewdrop fall,
Thenceforth to grow a jewel fit for courts,
And shine on swanlike necks of haughty queens!

But Krishna's third handmaiden scarce had felt
The fume from parchèd plains that made the air
As one vast caldron of invisible fire,
Than casting downward pitiful eyes, she saw,
Crouched in the brazen cere of that red heat,
A tiny bird—a poor, weak, suffering thing—
(Its bright eyes glazed, its limbs convulsed and
    prone),
Dying of thirst in torture: "Ah, kind Lord
Krishna," his handmaid murmured, "speed thy gift,
Best yielded here, to soothe, perchance to save,
The lowliest mortal creature cursed with pain!"
Gently she shook the dewdrop from her palm
Into the silent throat that thirst had sealed,
Soon silent, sealed no more,—for, lo! the bird
Fluttered, arose, was strengthened, and through calms

Of happy ether, echoing fair and far,
Rang the charmed music of the nightingale.

And so, where crowned beneath the mystic stars,
Nigh the twin founts of Immortality,
Krishna, the father, saw what ruth was hers,
And, smiling, to his wise handmaiden's rule
Gave the great storm-clouds and the mists of heaven,
Till at her voice the mighty vapors rolled
Up from the mountain-gorges, and the seas,
And cloud-land darkened, and the grateful rain,
Burdened with benedictions, rushed and foamed
Down the hot channels, and the foliaged hills,
And the frayed lips, and languid limbs of flowers;
And all the woodlands laughed, and earth was glad !

UNDER THE PINE.

TO THE MEMORY OF HENRY TIMROD.

THE same majestic Pine is lifted high
    Against the twilight sky,
The same low, melancholy music grieves
    Amid the topmost leaves,
As when I watched, and mused, and dreamt with him,
    Beneath these shadows dim.

O Tree ! hast thou no memory at thy core
    Of one who comes no more ?

No yearning memory of those scenes that were
    So richly calm and fair,
When the last rays of sunset, shimmering down,
    Flashed like a royal crown?

And he, with hand outstretched and eyes ablaze,
    Looked forth with burning gaze,
And seemed to drink the sunset like strong wine,
    Or, hushed in trance divine,
Hailed the first shy and tremulous glance from far
    Of Evening's virgin star?

O Tree! against thy mighty trunk he laid
    His weary head; thy shade
Stole o'er him like the first cool spell of sleep:
    It brought a peace *so* deep
The unquiet passion died from out his eyes,
    As lightning from stilled skies.

And in that calm he loved to rest, and hear
    The soft wind-angels, clear
And sweet, among the uppermost branches sighing:
    Voices he heard replying
(Or so he dreamed) far up the mystic height,
    And pinions rustling light.

O Tree! have not his poet-touch, his dreams
    So full of heavenly gleams,
Wrought through the folded dullness of thy bark,
    And all thy nature dark
Stirred to slow throbbings, and the fluttering fire
    Of faint, unknown desire?

At least to me there sweeps no rugged ring
    That girds the forest-king,
No immemorial stain, or awful rent
    (The mark of tempests spent),
No delicate leaf, no lithe bough, vine-o'ergrown,
    No distant, flickering cone,

But speaks of him, and seems to bring once more
    The joy, the love of yore;
But most when breathed from out the sunset-land
    The sunset airs are bland,
That blow between the twilight and the night,
    Ere yet the stars are bright;

For then that quiet eve comes back to me,
    When, deeply, thrillingly,
He spake of lofty hopes which vanquish Death;
    And on his mortal breath
A language of immortal meanings hung,
    That fired his heart and tongue.

For then unearthly breezes stir and sigh,
    Murmuring, "Look up! 'tis I:
Thy friend is near thee! Ah, thou canst not see!"
    And through the sacred Tree
Passes what seems a wild and sentient thrill—
    Passes, and all is still!—

Still as the grave which holds his tranquil form,
    Hushed after many a storm,—
Still as the calm that crowns his marble brow,
    No pain can wrinkle now,—
Still as the peace—pathetic peace of God—
    That wraps the holy sod,

Where every flower from our dead minstrel's dust
    Should bloom, a type of trust,—
That faith which waxed to wings of heavenward might
    To bear his soul from night,—
That faith, dear Christ! whereby we pray to meet
    His spirit at God's feet!

A DREAM OF THE SOUTH WIND.

    O FRESH, how fresh and fair
    Through the crystal gulfs of air,
The fairy South Wind floateth on her subtle wings of
    balm!
    And the green earth lapped in bliss,
    To the magic of her kiss
Seems yearning upward fondly through the golden-
    crested calm!

    From the distant Tropic strand,
    Where the billows, bright and bland,
Go creeping, curling round the palms with sweet, faint
    undertune,
    From its fields of purpling flowers,
    Still wet with fragrant showers,
The happy South Wind lingering sweeps the royal
    blooms of June.

    All heavenly fancies rise
    On the perfume of her sighs,

Which steep the inmost spirit in a languor rare and fine,
  And a Peace more pure than Sleep's
  Unto dim, half-conscious deeps,
Transports me, lulled and dreaming, on its twilight tides divine.

  Those dreams! ah me! the splendor,
  So mystical and tender,
Wherewith like soft heat-lightnings they gird their meaning round,
  And those waters, calling, calling,
  With a nameless charm enthralling,
Like the ghost of music melting on a rainbow spray of sound!

  Touch, touch me not, nor wake me,
  Lest grosser thoughts o'ertake me,
From earth receding faintly with her dreary din and jars,—
  What viewless arms caress me?
  What whispered voices bless me,
With welcomes dropping dewlike from the weird and wondrous stars?

  Alas! dim, dim, and dimmer
  Grows the preternatural glimmer
Of that trance the South Wind brought me on her subtle wings of balm,
  For behold! its spirit flieth,
  And its fairy murmur dieth,
And the silence closing round me is a dull and soulless calm!

AËTHRA.

It is a sweet tradition, with a soul
Of tenderest pathos! Hearken, love!—for all
The sacred undercurrents of the heart
Thrill to its cordial music:
                       Once, a chief,
Philantus, king of Sparta, left the stern
And bleak defiles of his unfruitful land—
Girt by a band of eager colonists—
To seek new homes on fair Italian plains.
Apollo's oracle had darkly spoken:
"*Where'er from cloudless skies a plenteous shower
Outpours, the Fates decree that ye should pause
And rear your household Deities!*" Racked by doubt
Philantus traversed with his faithful band
Full many a bounteous realm; but still defeat
Darkened his banners, and the strong-walled towns
His desperate sieges grimly laughed to scorn!
Weighed down by anxious thoughts, one sultry eve
The warrior—his rude helmet cast aside—
Rested his weary head upon the lap
Of his fair wife, who loved him tenderly;
And there he drank a generous draught of sleep.
She, gazing on his brow all worn with toil
And his dark locks, which pain had silvered over
With glistening touches of a frosty rime,
Wept on the sudden bitterly; her tears
Fell on his face, and, wondering, he awoke.

"O blest art thou, my Aëthra, *my clear sky*,"
He cried exultant, "from whose pitying blue
A heart-rain falls to fertilize my fate:
Lo! the deep riddle's solved—the gods spake truth!"

So the next night he stormed Tarentum, took
The enemy's host at vantage, and o'erthrew
His mightiest captains. Thence with kindly sway
He ruled those pleasant regions he had won,—
But dearer ever than his rich demesnes
The love of her whose gentle tears unlocked
The close-shut mystery of the Oracle!

IN THE MIST.

More fearful grows the hillside way,
   The gloom no softening breeze hath kissed!
I glance far upward to the Day,
But scarce can catch one faltering ray
     From out the mist!

Ah, heaven! to think youth's morning prime,
   All flushed with rose and amethyst,
Its tender loves, its hopes sublime,
Should shrink to this dull twilight-time
     Of cold and mist!

No tranquil evening Hour descends,
   When Peace with Memory holds her tryst,

But Doubt with prescient Terror blends,
And Grief her mournful curfew sends
    Along the mist!

Weird shapes and wild stalk strangely by,
    And say, what bodeful voices hissed
Where yonder blasted pine-trunks lie?
What mystic phantoms shuddering fly
    Far down the mist?

Dark omens all! they bid me stay,
    Unsheathe resolve, pause, strive, resist
That poisonous Charm which haunts my way;
Alas! the Fiend, more bold than they,
    Still rules the mist!

And now from gulfs of turbulent gloom
    A torrent's threatening thunder;—list!
That ravening roar! that hungry boom!
Down, down I pass to meet my doom
    Within the mist!

THE BONNY BROWN HAND.

Oh, drearily, how drearily, the sombre eve comes down!
And wearily, how wearily, the seaward breezes blow!
But place your little hand in mine—so dainty, yet so brown!
For household toil hath worn away its rosy-tinted snow;

But I fold it, wife, the nearer,
And I feel, my love, 'tis dearer
Than all dear things of earth,
As I watch the pensive gloaming,
And my wild thoughts cease from roaming,
And birdlike furl their pinions close beside our peaceful hearth:
Then rest your little hand in mine, while twilight shimmers down,—
That little hand, that fervent hand, that hand of bonny brown,—
The hand that holds an honest heart, and rules a happy hearth.

Oh, merrily, how merrily, our children's voices rise!
And cheerily, how cheerily, their tiny footsteps fall!
But, hand, you must not stir awhile, for there our nestling lies,
Snug in the cradle at your side, the loveliest far of all;
And she looks so arch and airy,
So softly pure a fairy,—
She scarce seems bound to earth;
And her dimpled mouth keeps smiling,
As at some child-fay's beguiling,
Who flies from Ariel realms to light her slumbers on the hearth.
Ha, little hand, you yearn to move, and smooth the bright locks down!
But, little hand,—but, trembling hand,—but, hand of bonny brown,
Stay, stay with me!—she will not flee, our birdling on the hearth.

Oh, flittingly, how flittingly, the parlor-shadows thrill,
  As wittingly, half wittingly, they seem to pulse and pass!
And solemn sounds are on the wind that sweeps the haunted hill,
  And murmurs of a ghostly breath from out the graveyard grass.
      Let me feel your glowing fingers
      In a clasp that warms and lingers
      With the full, fond love of earth,
      Till the joy of love's completeness
      In this flush of fireside sweetness,
Shall brim our hearts with spirit-wine, outpoured beside the hearth.
So steal your little hand in mine, while twilight falters down,—
That little hand, that fervent hand, that hand of bonny brown,—
The hand which points the path to heaven, yet makes a heaven of earth.

A SUMMER MOOD.

"Now, by my faith, a *gruesome* MOOD, for summer!"—THOMAS HEYWARD (1597).

AH! me, for evermore, for evermore
  These human hearts of ours must yearn and sigh,
While down the dells and up the murmurous shore
  Nature renews her immortality.

A SUMMER MOOD.

The heavens of June stretch calm and bland above,
    June roses blush with tints of Orient skies,
But we, by graves of joy, desire, and love,
    Mourn in a world which breathes of Paradise!

The sunshine mocks the tears it may not dry,
    The breezes—tricksy couriers of the air,—
Child-roisterers winged, and lightly fluttering by—
    Blow their gay trumpets in the face of care;

And bolder winds, the deep sky's passionate speech,
    Woven into rhythmic raptures of desire,
Or fugues of mystic victory, sadly reach
    Our humbled souls, to rack, not raise them higher!

The field-birds seem to twit us as they pass
    With their small blisses, piped so clear and loud;
The cricket triumphs o'er us in the grass,
    And the lark, glancing beamlike up the cloud,

Sings us to scorn with his keen rhapsodies:
    Small things and great unconscious tauntings bring
To edge our cares, whilst we, the proud and wise,
    Envy the insect's joy, the birdling's wing!

And thus for evermore, till time shall cease,
    Man's soul and Nature's—each a separate sphere—
Revolves, the one in discord, one in peace,
    And who shall make the solemn mystery clear?

MIDNIGHT.

The Moon, a ghost of her sweet self,
   And wading through a watery cloud
   (Which wraps her lustre like a shroud),
Creeps up the gray, funereal sky,
          Wearily! how wearily!

The Wind, with low, bewildered wail
   (A homeless spirit, sadly lost),
   Sweeps shuddering o'er the pallid frost,
And faints afar, with heart-sick sigh,
          Drearily! how drearily!

And now a deathly stillness falls
   On Earth and Heaven, save when the shrill,
   Malignant owl o'er heath and hill
Smites the wan silence with a cry,
          Eerily! how eerily!

SONNET.

ADDRESSED TO WILLIAM MORRIS, AFTER READING HIS "L'ENVOY," IN THE THIRD VOLUME OF HIS "EARTHLY PARADISE."

In some fair realm unbound of time or space,
Where souls of all dead May-times, with their play
Of blissful winds, soft showers, and bird-notes gay,
Make mystic music in the flower-bright place,—
Yea, there, O poets!* radiant face to face,
Keen heart to heart, beneath the enchanted day,
Ye met, each hearkening to the other's lay,
With rapt, sweet eyes, and thoughts of Old-World grace:
"Son," saith the elder bard, "when thou wert born,
So yearned toward thine my spirit's fervency,
Flamelike its warmth on thy deep soul was shed;
Hence the ripe blood of England's lustier morn
Of song burns through thee; hence alone on thee
Fall the rich bays which bloomed round Chaucer's head!"

---

* Chaucer and the author of "The Earthly Paradise."

SONNET.

NOVEMBER.

Within the deep-blue eyes of Heaven a haze
Of saddened passion dims their tender light,
For that her fair queen-child, the Summer bright,
Lies a wan corse amidst her mouldering bays:
The sullen Autumn lifts no voice of praise
To herald Winter's cold and cruel might,
But winds foreboding fill the desolate night,
And die at dawning down wild woodland ways:
The sovereign sun at noonday smileth cold,
As through a shroud he hath no power to part,
While huddled flocks crouch listless round their fold;
The mock-bird's dumb, no more with cheerful dart
Upsoars the lark through morning's quivering gold,
And dumb or dead, methinks, great Nature's heart!

SONNET.

SYLVAN MUSINGS.

IN MAY.

Couched in cool shadow, girt by billowy swells
Of foliage, rippling into buds and flowers,
Here I repose o'erfanned by breezy bowers,—
Lulled by a delicate stream whose music wells

Tender and low through those luxuriant dells,
Wherefrom a single broad-leaved chestnut towers;—
Still musing in the long, lush, languid hours,—
As in a dream I heard the tinkling bells
Of far-off kine, glimpsed through the verdurous sheen,
Blent with faint bleatings from the distant croft,—
The bee-throngs murmurous in the golden fern,
The wood-doves veiled by depths of flickering green,—
And near me, where the wild "queen fairies"* burn,
The thrush's bridal passion, warm and soft!

SONNET.

THE COTTAGE ON THE HILL.

On a steep hillside, to all airs that blow,
Open, and open to the varying sky,
Our cottage homestead, smiling tranquilly,
Catches morn's earliest and eve's latest glow;
Here, far from worldly strife, and pompous show,
The peaceful seasons glide serenely by,
Fulfill their missions, and as calmly die,
As waves on quiet shores when winds are low.
Fields, lonely paths, the one small glimmering rill
That twinkles like a wood-fay's mirthful eye,
Under moist bay-leaves, clouds fantastical
That float and change at the light breeze's will,—
To me, thus lapped in sylvan luxury,
Are more than death of kings, or empires' fall.

---

* "Queen fairies," the name given popularly to an exquisite Southern wild-flower.

SONNET.

POETS.

Some thunder on the heights of song, their race
Godlike in power, while others at their feet
Are breathing measures scarce less strong and sweet
Than those which peal from out that loftiest place;
Meantime, just midway on the mount, his face
Fairer than April heavens, when storms retreat,
And on their edges rain and sunshine meet,
Pipes the soft lyrist lays of tender grace;
But where the slopes of bright Parnassus sweep
Near to the common ground, a various throng
Chant lowlier measures,—yet each tuneful strain
(The silvery minor of earth's perfect song)
Blends with that music of the topmost steep,
O'er whose vast realm the master minstrels reign!

SONNET.

THE PHANTOM BELLS.

Upveiled in yonder dim ethereal sea,
Its airy towers the work of phantom spells,
A viewless belfry tolls its wizard bells,
Pealed o'er this populous earth perpetually.

Some hear, some hear them not; but aye they be
Laden with one strange note that sinks or swells,
Now dread as doom, now gentle as farewells,—
Time's dirge borne ever toward eternity.
Each hour its measured breath sobs out and dies,
While the bells toll its requiem,—"*Passing, past,*"—
The sole sad burden of their long refrain.
Still, with those hours each pang, each pleasure flies,
Brief sweet, brief bitter,—all our days are vain,
Knolled into drear forgetfulness at last.

SONNET.

BEHOLD! how weirdly, wonderfully grand
The shapes and colors of yon sunset sky!
Rare isles of light in crimson oceans lie,
Whose airy waves seem rippling, bright and bland,
Up the soft slopes of many a mystic strand,—
While luminous capes, and mountains towering high
In golden pomp and proud regality,
O'erlook the frontiers of that fairy-land,—
But now, in transformations swift and strange
The vision changes! Castles, glittering fair,
And sapphire battlements of loftiest range
Commingle with vast spire and gorgeous dome,
Round which the sunset rolls its purpling foam,
Girding this transient VENICE of the air.

SONNET.

THE LIFE-FOREST.

In Springtime of our youth life's purpling shade,
Foliage and fruit, do hang so thickly round;
We seem glad tenants of enchanted ground,
O'er which for aye dream-whispering winds have played.
Then Summer comes,—her full-blown charm is laid
On all the forest aisles; from bound to bound
Floats woodland music, and the silvery sound
Of fountains babbling to the golden glade.
Next, a chill breath, the breath of Autumn's doom
Strips the fair sylvan branches, one by one,
Till the bared landscape broadens to our view;
Behind, black tree-boles blot the twilight blue,
Before, unfoliaged, bald of light and bloom,
  Our pathway darkens towards the darkening sun!

SONNET.

CLOUD-FANTASIES.

Wild, rapid, dark, like dreams of threatening doom,
Low cloud-racks scud before the level wind;
Beneath them, the bared moorlands, blank and blind,
Stretch, mournful, through pale lengths of glimmering
    gloom;
Afar, grand mimic of the sea-waves' boom,
Hollow, yet sweet, as if a Titan pined

O'er deathless woes, yon mighty wood consigned
To Autumn's blight, bemoans its perished bloom;
The dim air creeps with a vague, shuddering thrill
Down from those monstrous mists, the sea-gale brings,
Half formless, inland, poisoning earth and sky;
Most from yon black cloud, shaped like vampire wings
O'er a lost angel's visage, deathly-still,
Uplifted toward some dread eternity.

SONNET.

OF all the woodland flowers of earlier spring,
These golden jasmines, each an air-hung bower,
Meet for the Queen of Fairies' tiring hour,
Seem loveliest and most fair in blossoming;—
How yonder mock-bird thrills his fervid wing
And long, lithe throat, where twinkling flower on flower
Rains the globed dewdrops down, a diamond shower,
O'er his brown head, poised as in act to sing;—
Lo! the swift sunshine floods the flowery urns,
Girding their delicate gold with matchless light,
Till the blent life of bough, leaf, blossom, burns;
Then, then outbursts the mock-bird clear and loud,
Half-drunk with perfume, veiled by radiance bright,—
A star of music in a fiery cloud!

SONNET.

I FEAR thee not, O Death! nay, oft I pine
To clasp thy passionless bosom to mine own,—
And on thy heart sob out my latest moan,
Ere lapped and lost in thy strange sleep divine;
But much I fear lest that chill breath of thine
Should freeze all tender memories into stone,—
Lest ruthless and malign Oblivion
Quench the last spark that lingers on love's shrine:—
O God! to moulder through dark, dateless years,—
The while all loving ministries shall cease,
And Time assuage the fondest mourner's tears!—
Here lies the sting!—this, *this* it is to die!—
And yet great Nature rounds all strife with peace,
And life or death,—each rests in mystery!

FIRE-PICTURES.

O! THE rolling, rushing Fire!
    O! the Fire!
How it rages, wilder, higher,
Like a hot heart's fierce desire,
Thrilled with passion that appalls us,
Half appalls, and yet enthralls us,
    O! the madly mounting Fire!

FIRE PICTURES.

Up it sweepeth,—wave and quiver,—
Roaring like an angry river,—
    O! the Fire!—
Which an earthquake backward turneth,
Backward o'er its riven courses,
Backward to its mountain sources,
While the blood-red sunset burneth,
Like a God's face grand with ire,—
    O! the bursting, billowy Fire!

Now the sombre smoke-clouds thicken
To a dim Plutonian night;—
    O! the Fire!—
How its flickering glories sicken,
Sicken at the blight!
Pales the flame, and spreads the vapor,
Till scarce larger than a taper,
Flares the waning, struggling light:
O! thou wan, faint-hearted Fire,
    Sadly darkling,
    Weakly sparkling,
    Rise! assert thy might!
    Aspire! aspire!

At the word, a vivid lightning,
Threat'ning, swaying, darting, bright'ning,
Where the loftiest yule-log towers,—
    Bursts once more,
Sudden bursts the awakened Fire;
    Hear it roar!
Roar, and mount high, high, and higher,
    Till beneath,
Only here and there a wreath

Of the passing smoke-cloud lowers,—
Ha! the glad, victorious Fire!

O! the Fire!
How it changes,
Changes, ranges
Through all phases fancy-wrought,
Changes like a wizard thought;
See Vesuvian lavas rushing
'Twixt the rocks! the ground asunder
Shivers at the earthquake's thunder,
And the glare of Hell is flushing
Startled hill-top, quaking town;
Temples, statues, towers go down,
While beyond that lava-flood,
Dark-red like blood,
I behold the children fleeting
Clasped by many a frenzied hand;
What a flight, and what a meeting,
On the ruined strand!

O! the Fire!
Eddying higher, higher, higher
From the vast volcanic cones;
O! the agony, the groans
Of those thousands stifling there!
"Fancy," say you? but how near
Seem the anguish and the fear!

Swelling, turbulent, pitiless Fire:
'Tis a mad northeastern breeze
Raving o'er the prairie seas;
How, like living things, the grasses
Tremble as the storm-breath passes,

Ere the flames' devouring magic
Coils about their golden splendor,
    And the tender
Glory of the mellowing fields
To the wild Destroyer yields;
Dreadful waste for flowering blooms,
Desolate darkness, like the tomb's,
Over which there broods the while,
Instead of daylight's happy smile,
A pall malign and tragic!

    Marvelous Fire!
    Changing, ranging
Through all phases fancy-wrought,
Changing like a charmèd thought;
A stir, a murmur deep,
Like airs that rustle over jungle-reeds,
Where the gaunt Tiger breathes but half asleep;
    A bodeful stir,—
And then the victim of his own pure deeds,
    I mark the mighty Fire
Clasp in its cruel palms a martyr-saint,
    Christ's faithful worshiper;—
One mortal cry affronts the pitying Day,
One ghastly arm uplifts itself to heaven—
When the swart smoke is riven,—
Ere the last sob of anguish dies away,
The worn limbs droop and faint,
And o'er those reverend hairs, silvered and hoary,
Settles the semblance of a crown of glory.

    Tireless Fire!
    Changing, ranging

Through all phases fancy-wrought,
Changing like a Prótean thought;
Here's a glowing, warm interior,
A Dutch tavern, rich and rosy
With deep color,—sill and floor
Dazzling as the white seashore,
Where within his arm-chair cosy
Sits a Toper, stout and yellow,
Blinking o'er his steamy bowl;
   Hugely drinking,
   Slyly winking,
As the pot-house Hebé passes,
With a clink and clang of glasses;
Ha! 'tis plain, the stout old fellow—
As his wont is—waxes mellow,
Nodding 'twixt each dreamy leer,
Swaying in his elbow chair,
Next to one,—a portly Peasant,—
Pipe in hand, whose swelling cheek,
Jolly, rubicund, and sleek,
Puffs above the blazing coal;
While his heavy, half-shut eyes
Watch the smoke wreaths evanescent,
Eddying lightly as they rise,
Eddying lightly and aloof
Toward the great, black, oaken roof!

Dreaming still, from out the Fire
Faces grinning and grotesque,
Flash an eery glance upon me;
Or, once more, methinks, I sun me
On the breadths of happy plain
Sloping towards the Southern main,

Where the inmost soul of shadow
      Wins a golden heat,
And the hill-side and the meadow
(Where the vines and clover meet,
Twining round the virgins' feet,
While the natural arabesque
Of the foliage grouped above them
Droops, as if the leaves did love them,
Over brow, and lips, and eyes)
Gleam with hints of Paradise!

      Ah! the Fire!
      Gently glowing,
      Fairly flowing,
Like a rivulet rippling deep
Through the meadow-lands of sleep,
Bordered where its music swells,
By the languid lotos-bells,
And the twilight asphodels;
Mingled with a richer boon
Of queen-lilies, each a moon,
Orbèd into white completeness;
O! the perfume! the rare sweetness
Of those grouped and fairy flowers,
Over which the love-lorn hours
Linger,—not alone for them,
Though the lotos swings its stem
With a lulling stir of leaves,—
Though the lady-lily laves
Coy feet in the crystal waves,
And a silvery undertune
From some mystic wind-song grieves

Dainty-sweet, amid the bells
Of the twilight asphodels;
But because a charm more rare
Glorifies the mellow air,
In the gleam of lifted eyes,
In the tranquil ecstasies
Of two lovers, leaf-embowered,
      Lingering there,—
Each of whose fair lives hath flowered,
Like the lily-petals finely,
Like the asphodel divinely.

      Titan arches!
      Titan spires!
Pillars whose vast capitals
Tower towards Cyclopean halls,
And whose unknown bases pierce
Down the nether Universe;
Countless coruscations glimmer,
Glow and darken, wane and shimmer,
'Twixt majestic standards, swooping,—
Like the wings of some strange bird
By mysterious currents stirred
Of great winds,—or darkly drooping,—
In a hush sublime as death,
When the conflict's quivering breath
Sobs its gory life away,
At the close of fateful marches,
On an empire's natal day:
Countless coruscations glimmer,
Glow and darken, wane and shimmer,
Round the shafts, and round the walls,
Whence an ebon splendor falls

On the scar-seamed, angel bands,—
    (Desolate bands!)
Grasping in their ghostly hands
Weapons of an antique rage,
From some lost, celestial age,
When the serried throngs were hurled
Blasted to the under world:
Shattered spear-heads, broken brands,
And the mammoth, moonlike shields,
Blazoned on their lurid fields,
With uncouth, malignant forms,
    Glowering, wild,
Like the huge cloud-masses piled
Up a Heaven of storms!
*   *   *   *   *   *   *

Ah, the faint and flickering Fire!
    Ah, the Fire!
Like a young man's transient ire,
Like an old man's last desire,
Lo! it falters, dies!
Still, through weary, half-closed lashes,
    Still I see,
  But brokenly, but mistily,
    Fall and rise,
    Rise and fall,
  Ghosts of shifting phantasy;
Now the embers, smouldered all,
Sink to ruin; sadder dreams
Follow on their vanished gleams;
Wailingly the spirits call,
Spirits on the night-winds solemn,
Wraiths of happy Hopes that left me;

(Cruel! why did ye depart?)
Hopes that sleep, their youthful riot
Mergèd in an awful quiet,
With the heavy grief-moulds pressed
On each pallid, pulseless breast,
In that graveyard called THE HEART,
    Stern and lone,
  Needing no memorial stone,
  And no blazoned column:
    Let them rest!
    Let them rest!
Yes, 'tis useless to remember
May-morn in the mirk December;
Still, O Hopes! because ye were
Beautiful, and strong, and fair,
Nobly brave, and sweetly bright,
    Who shall dare
Scorn me, if through moistened lashes,
Musing by my hearthstone blighted,
Weary, desolate, benighted,—
I, because those sweet Hopes left me,
I, because my Fate bereft me,
    Mourn my dead,
    Mourn,—and shed
  Hot tears in the ashes?

FROM THE WOODS.

Why should I, with a mournful, morbid spleen,
Lament that here, in this half-desert scene,
    My lot is placed?
At least the poet-winds are bold and loud,—
At least the sunset glorifies the cloud,
    And forests old and proud
Rustle their verdurous banners o'er the waste.

Perchance 'tis best that I, whose Fate's eclipse
Seems final,—I, whose sluggish life-wave slips
    Languid away,—
Should here, within these lowly walks, apart
From the fierce throbbings of the populous mart,
    Commune with mine own heart,
While Wisdom blooms from buried Hope's decay.

Nature, though wild her forms, sustains me still;
The founts are musical,—the barren hill
    Glows with strange lights;
Through solemn pine-groves the small rivulets fleet
Sparkling, as if a Naiad's silvery feet,
    In quick and coy retreat,
Glanced through the star-gleams on calm summer nights;

And the great sky, the royal heaven above,
Darkens with storms or melts in hues of love;
    While far remote,

Just where the sunlight smites the woods with fire,
Wakens the multitudinous sylvan choir;
    There innocent love's desire
Poured in a rill of song from each harmonious throat.

My walls are crumbling, but immortal looks
Smile on me here from faces of rare books:
    Shakspeare consoles
My heart with true philosophies; a balm
Of spiritual dews from humbler song or psalm
    Fills me with tender calm,
Or through hushed heavens of soul Milton's deep thunder rolls!

And more than all, o'er shattered wrecks of Fate,
The relics of a happier time and state,
    My nobler Life
Shines on unquenched! O deathless love that lies
In the clear midnight of those passionate eyes!
    Joy waneth! Fortune flies!
What then? Thou still art here, soul of my soul, my Wife!

AN ANNIVERSARY.

O Love, it is our wedding-day!
  This morn,—how swift the seasons flee!—
A virgin morn of cloudless May,
  You gave your loyal hand to me,
Your dainty hand, claspt sweet and sure
As Love's sweet self, for evermore!

AN ANNIVERSARY.

O Love, it is our wedding-day,
   And memory flies from now to then;
I mark the soft heat-lightning play
   Of blushes o'er your cheek again,
And shy but fond foreshadowings rise
Of tranquil joy in tender eyes.

O Love, it is our wedding-day;
   The very rustling of your dress,
The trembling of your arm that lay
   On mine, with timorous happiness,
Your fluttered breath and faint footfall,—
Ah, sweet, I hear, I see them all!

O Love, it is our wedding-day,
   And backward Time's strange current rolls,
Till life's and love's auspicious May
   Once more is blooming in our souls,
And, larklike, swell the songs of hope,
Your blissful bridal horoscope.

O Love, it is our wedding-day,—
   Yet say, did those fair hopes but sing,
Lapped in the tuneful morn of May,
   To die or droop on faltering wing,
When noontide heats and evening chills
Made pale the flowers and veiled the hills?

O Love, it is our wedding-day,
   And none of those glad hopes of youth,
Thrilled to its height, outpoured a lay
   To match our future's simple truth:
Though deep the joy of vow and shrine,
Our wedded calm is more divine!

O Love, it is our wedding-day!
  Life's summer, with slow-waning beam,
Tints the near autumn's cloud-land gray
  To softness of a fairy dream,
Whence Peace by musing Pathos kissed,
Smiles through a veil of golden mist.

O Love, it is our wedding-day;
  The conscious winds are whispering low
Those passionate secrets of the May
  Fraught with your kisses long ago;
Warm memories of our years remote
Are trembling in the mock-bird's throat.

O Love, it is our wedding-day,—
  And not a thrush in woodland bowers,
And not a rivulet's silvery lay,
  Nor tiny bee-song 'mid the flowers,
Nor any voice of land or sea,
But deepens love to ecstasy!

Our wedding-day! The soul's noontide!
  In these rare words at watchful rest
What sweet, melodious meanings hide
  Like birds within one balmy nest,
Each quivering with an impulse strong
To flood all heaven and earth with song!

DOLCE FAR NIENTE.

LET the world roll blindly on !
Give me shadow, give me sun,
And a perfumed eve as this is :
    Let me lie,
    Dreamfully,
When the last quick sunbeams shiver
Spears of light athwart the river,
And a breeze, which seems the sigh
Of a fairy floating by,
    Coyly kisses
Tender leaf and feathered grasses;
Yet so soft its breathing passes,
These tall ferns, just glimmering o'er me,
Blending goldenly before me,
    Hardly quiver !

I have done with worldly scheming,
Mocking show, and hollow seeming !
    Let me lie
    Idly here,
Lapped in lulling waves of air,
Facing full the shadowy sky.
Fame !—the very sound is dreary,—
Shut, O soul ! thine eyelids weary,
For all nature's voices say,
"'Tis the close—the close of day,
Thought and grief have had their sway:"

Now Sleep bares her balmy breast,—
    Whispering low
(Low as moon-set tides that flow
Up still beaches far away;
While, from out the lucid West,
Flutelike winds of murmurous breath
Sink to tender-panting death),
"On my bosom take thy rest;
(Care and grief have had their day!)
'Tis the hour for dreaming,
Fragrant rest, elysian dreaming!"

CAMBYSES AND THE MACROBIAN BOW.

ONE morn, hard by a slumberous streamlet's wave,
The plane-trees stirless in the unbreathing calm,
And all the lush-red roses drooped in dream,
Lay King Cambyses, idle as a cloud
That waits the wind,—aimless of thought and will,—
But with vague evil, like the lightning's bolt
Ere yet the electric death be forged to smite,
Seething at heart. His courtiers ringed him round,
Whereof was one who to his comrades' ears,
With bated breath and wonder-archèd brows,
Extolled a certain Bactrian's matchless skill
Displayed in bowcraft: at whose marvelous feats,
Eagerly vaunted, the King's soul grew hot
With envy, for himself erewhile had been
Rated the mightiest archer in his realm.

Slowly he rose, and pointing southward, said,
"Seest thou, Prexaspes, yonder slender palm,
A mere wan shadow quivering in the light,
Topped by a ghostly leaf-crown? Prithee, now,
Can this, thy famous Bactrian, standing here,
Cleave with his shaft a hand's breadth marked thereon?"
To which Prexaspes answered, "Nay, my lord;
I spake of feats compassed by mortal skill,
Not of Gods' prowess." Unto whom, the King:—
"And if myself, Prexaspes, made essay,
Think'st thou, wise counselor, I too should fail?"
"Needs *must* I, sire,"—albeit the courtier's voice
Trembled, and some dark prescience bade him pause,—
"Needs must I hold such cunning more than man's;
And for the rest, I pray thy pardon, King,
But yester-eve, amid the feast and dance,
Thou tarried'st with the beakers overlong."

The thick, wild, treacherous eyebrows of the King,
That looked a sheltering ambush for ill thoughts
Waxing to manhood of malignant acts,—
These treacherous eyebrows, pent-house fashion, closed
O'er the black orbits of his fiery eyes,—
Which, clouded thus, but flashed a deadlier gleam
On all before him: suddenly as fire,
Half choked and smouldering in its own dense smoke,
Bursts into roaring radiance and swift flame,
Touched by keen breaths of liberating wind,—
So now Cambyses' eyes a stormy joy
Stormily filled; for on Prexaspes' son,

His first-born son, they lingered,—a fair boy
('Mid most his fellow-pages flushed with sport),
Who, in his office of King's cup-bearer,—
So gracious and so sweet were all his ways,—
Had even the captious sovereign seemed to please;
While for the court, the reckless, reveling court,
They loved him one and all:
"Go," said Cambyses now, his voice a hiss,
Poisonous, and low, "go, bind my dainty page
To yonder palm-tree; bind him fast and sure,
So that no finger stirreth; which being done,
Fetch me, Prexaspes, the Macrobian bow."

Thus ordered, thus accomplished, fast they bound
The innocent child, the while that mammoth bow,
Brought by the spies from Ethiopian camps,
Lay in the King's hand; slowly, sternly up,
He reared it to the level of his sight,
Reared, and bent back its oaken massiveness
Till the vast muscles, tough as grapevines, bulged
From naked arm and shoulder, and the horns
Of the fierce weapon groaning, almost met,
When, with one lowering glance askance at him,—
His doubting Satrap,—the King coolly said,
"*Prexaspes, look, my aim is at the heart!*"

Then came the sharp twang, and the deadly whirr
Of the loosed arrow, followed by the dull,
Drear echo of a bolt that smites its mark;
And those of keenest vision shook to see
The fair child fallen forward across his bonds,
With all his limbs a-quivering. Quoth the King,
Clapping Prexaspes' shoulder, as in glee,

"Go thou, and tell me how that shaft hath sped!"
Forward the wretched father, step by step,
Crept, as one creeps whom black Hadèan dreams,
Visions of fate and fear unutterable,
Draw, tranced and rigid, towards some definite goal
Of horror; thus he went, and thus he saw
What never in the noontide or the night,
Awake or sleeping, idle or in toil,
'Neath the wild forest or the perfumed lamps
Of palaces, shall leave his stricken sight
Unblasted, or his spirit purged of woe.

Prexaspes saw, yet lived; saw, and returned
Where still environed by his dissolute court,
Cambyses leaned, half scornful, on his bow:
The old man's face was riven and white as death;
But making meek obeisance to his King,
He smiled (ah, *such* a smile!) and feebly said,
"What *am* I, mighty master, what am *I*,
That I durst question my lord's strength and skill?
His arrows are like arrows of the god,
Egyptian Horus,—and for proof,—but now,
I felt a child's heart (once the child was *mine*,
'Tis my Lord's now and Death's), all mute and still,
Pierced by his shaft, and cloven, ye gods! in twain!"

Then laughed the great King loudly, till his beard
Quivered, and all his stalwart body shook
With merriment; but when his mirth was calmed,
"Thou art forgiven," said he, "forgiven, old man;
Only when next these Persian dogs shall call
Cambyses drunkard, rise, Prexaspes, rise!
And tell them how, and to what purpose, once,

Once, on a morn which followed hot and wan
A night of monstrous revel and debauch,—
Cambyses bent this huge Macrobian bow."

BY THE AUTUMN SEA.

FAIR as the dawn of the fairest day,
Sad as the evening's tender gray,
By the latest lustre of sunset kissed,
That wavers and wanes through an ámber mist,—
There cometh a dream of the past to me,
On the desert sands, by the autumn sea.

All heaven is wrapped in a mystic veil,
And the face of the ocean is dim and pale,
And there rises a wind from the chill northwest,
That seemeth the wail of a soul's unrest,
As the twilight falls, and the vapors flee
Far over the wastes of the autumn sea.

A single ship through the gloaming glides
Upborne on the swell of the seaward tides;
And above the gleam of her topmost spar
Are the virgin eyes of the vesper-star
That shine with an angel's ruth on me,—
A hopeless waif, by the autumn sea.

The wings of the ghostly beach-birds gleam
Through the shimmering surf, and the curlew's scream

Falls faintly shrill from the darkening height;
The first weird sigh on the lips of Night
Breathes low through the sedge and the blasted tree,
With a murmur of doom, by the autumn sea.

Oh, sky-enshadowed and yearning main,
Your gloom but deepens this *human* pain;
Those waves seem big with a nameless care,
That sky is a type of the heart's despair,
As I linger and muse by the sombre lea,
And the night-shades close on the autumn sea.

THE WIFE OF BRITTANY.

(SUGGESTED BY THE FRANKELEINES TALE OF CHAUCER.)

PROEM.

TRUTH wed to beauty in an antique tale,
Sweet-voiced like some immortal nightingale,
Trills the clear burden of her passionate lay,
As fresh, as fair, as wonderful to-day,
As when the music of her balmy tongue
Ravished the first warm hearts for whom she sung.

Thus, when the early spring-dawn buds are green,
Glistening beneath the sudden silvery sheen

Of glancing showers; while heaven with bridegroom-kiss
Wakens the virgin earth to bloom and bliss,
Enamored breathing, and soft raptures born
About the roseate footsteps of the morn,—
An old-world song, whose breezy music pours
Through limpid channels 'twixt enchanted shores,
Steals on me wooingly from that far time
When tuneful Chaucer wrought his lusty rhyme
Into rare shapes of fancy and delight,
For May winds blithely blew, and hawthorn flowers were bright.

O brave old poet! genius frank and bold!
Sustain me, cherish, and around me fold
Thine own hale, sun-warm atmosphere of song,
Lest I, who touch thy numbers, do thee wrong;
Speed the deep measure, make the meaning shine
Ruddy and high with healthful spirit-wine,
Till to attempered sense and quickening ears
My strain some faint harmonious echo bears
From that rich realm wherein thy cordial art
Throbbed with its pulse of fire 'gainst youthful England's heart.

THE STORY.

Where the hoarse billows of the Northland Sea
Sweep the rude coast of rock-bound Brittany,
Dwelt, ages since, a knight, whose warrior-fame
Might well have struck all carpet-knights with shame;
Vowed to great deeds and princely manhood, he
Burgeoned the topmost flower of chivalry;

Yet gentle-hearted, nursed one delicate thought
Fixed firm in love: with anxious pain he sought
To serve his lady in the noblest wise,
And many a labor, many a grand emprise
He wrought ere that sweet lady could be won.
She was a maiden bright-aired as the sun,
And graceful as the tall lake-lilies are
Flushed 'twixt the twilight and the vesper-star;
But born to such rare state and sovereignty,
He hardly durst before her bend the knee
In passion's ardor and keen heart-distress;
Still, at the last, his loyal worthiness
And mild obeisance, his observance high
Of manly faith, firm will, and constancy,
Aroused an answering pity to his sighs,
Till pity, grown to love, beamed forth from genial
    eyes.

Thus with pure trust, and cheerful calm accord,
She made this gentle suitor her soul's lord;
And he, that thence their happy fates should stray
Through pastures beauteous as the fields of May,
Swore of his own free mind to use the right
Her mercy gave him, with no churlish might,
Nor e'er in wanton freaks of mastery,
Ire-bred perverseness, or sharp jealousy,
Vex the clear-flowing current of her days.
She thanked him in a hundred winning ways:
"And I," she said, "will be thy loyal wife;
Take here my vows, my solemn troth for life."

On a June morning, when the verdurous woods
Flushed to the core of dew-lit solitudes,

Murmured almost as with a human feeling,
Tenderly low, to frolic breezes stealing
Through dappled shades and depths of dainty fern,
Crossed here and there by some low-whimpering burn,
These twain were wedded at a forest shrine.
O saffron-vested Hymen the divine!
Did aught of gloom or boding shadow weigh
Upon thy blushing consciousness that day?
No! thy frank face breathed only hope and love;
Earth laughed in wave and leaf, all heaven was fair
    above.

Home to the land wherein the knight was born
Blithely they rode upon the morrow-morn,
Not far from Penmark; there they lived in ease
And solace of matured felicities,
Until Arviragus whose soul of fire
Not even fruition of his love's desire
Could fill with languorous idlesse, cut the tie
Which bound to silken dalliance suddenly,
Sailing the straits for England's war-torn strand,
There ampler bays to pluck from victory's "red right
    hand."

But Iolene, fond Iolene, whose heart
Can beat no longer, lonely and apart
From him she loves, save with a sickening stress
Of fear o'erwrought and brooding tenderness,
Mourns for his absence with soul-wearying plaint,
Slow, pitiful tears and midnight murmurings faint,
And thus the whole world sadly sets at naught.
Meanwhile her friends, who guess what canker-thought
Preys on her quiet, with a mild essay

Strive to subdue her passion's torturing sway:
"Beware! beware, sweet lady, thou wilt slay
Thy reason! nay, thy very life's at stake!
By love, and love's dear pleadings, for his sake
Who yearns to clasp thee scathless to his breast,
We pray thee, soothe these maddening cares to rest!"

Even as the patient graver on a stone,
Laboring with tireless fingers, sees anon
The shape embodying his rare fancies grow
And lighten, thus upon her stubborn woe
Their tireless comforts wrought, until a Trust,
Clear-eyed and constant, raised her from the dust
And ashy shroud of sorrow; her despair
Gave place to twilight gladness and soft cheer,
Confirmed ere long by letters from her love:
"Dear Iolene!" he wrote, "thou tender dove
That tremblest in thy chilly nest at home,
Prithee embrace meek patience till I come.
Lo, the swift winds blow freshening o'er the sea,
From out the sunset isles I speed to rest with thee!"

The knight's ancestral home stood grim and tall
Beyond its shadowy moat and frowning wall;
It topped a gradual summit crowned with fir,
Green murmurous myrtle, and wild juniper,
Fronting a long, rude, solitary strand,
Whereon the earliest sunbeam, like a hand
Of tremulous benediction, rested bland,
And warmly quivering; o'er the wave-worn lea
Gleamed the broad spaces of the open sea.
Now often, with her pitying friends beside,
She walked the desolate beach and watched the tide,

Forth looking through unconscious tears to view
Sail after sail pass shimmering o'er the blue;
And to herself, ofttimes, "Alas!" said she,
"Is there no ship, of all these ships I see,
Will bring me home my lord? Woe, woe is me!
Though winds blow fresh, and sea-birds skim the main,
'Thou still delay'st, my liege! Ah, *wilt* thou come again?"

Sometimes would she, half-dreaming, sit and think,
Casting her dark eyes downward from the brink;
And when she saw those grisly rocks beneath,
Round which the pallid foam, in many a wreath
White as the lips of passion, faintly curled,
Her thoughts would pierce to the drear under-world,
'Mid shipwrecks wandering, and bleached bones of those
O'er whom the unresting ocean ebbs and flows;
And though the shining waters hushed and deep,
Might slumber like an innocent child asleep,
From out the North her prescient fancy raised
Huge ghostlike clouds, and spectral lightnings blazed
I' th' van of phantom thunder, and the roar
Of multitudinous waters on the shore,
Heard as in dreadful trance its billowy swells
Blent with the mournful tone of far funereal bells!

Her friends perceiving that this seaside walk,
Though gay and jovial their unstudied talk,
But dashed her dubious spirits, kindly took
And led her where the blossom-bordered brook
Babbled through woodlands, and the limpid pool
Lay couched like some shy Naiad in the cool

Of mossy glades; or when a tedious hour
Pressed on her with its dim, lethargic power,
They wooed her with glad games or jocund song,
Till the dull demon ceased to do her wrong.

So, on a pleasant May morn, while the dew
Sparkled on tiny hedgerow-flowers of blue,
Passing through many a sun-brown orchard-field,
They reach a fairy plesaunce, which revealed
Such prospects into breezy inland vales,
The natural haunt of plaining nightingales,
Such verdant, grassy plots, through which there rolled
A gleeful rivulet glimpsing sands of gold,
And winding slow by clumps of pluměd pines,
Rich realms of bay, and gorgeous jasmine-vines,
That none who strayed to that fair flowery place
Had paused in wonder if its sylvan Grace,
Embodied, beauteous, with an arch embrace
Had stopped, and smiling, kissed them face to face.

A buoyant, blithesome company were they,
Grouped round the plesaunce on that morn of May;
Wit, song, and rippling laughter, and arch looks
That might have lured the wood-gods from their nooks,
Echoed and flashed like dazzling arrows tipped
With amorous heat; and now and then there slipped
From out the whirling ring of jocund girls,
Wreathing white arms and tossing wanton curls,
Some maiden who with momentary mien
Of coy demureness bent o'er Iolene,
And whispered sunniest nothings in her ear.

First 'mid the brave gallants assembling there

Aurelian came, a squire of fair degree,
Tall, vigorous, handsome, his whole air so free,
Yet courteous, and such princely sweetness blent
With every well-timed, graceful compliment,
That sooth to speak, where'er Aurelian went,
To turbulent tilt-yard and baronial hall,
Sporting a-field or at high festival,
Favor, like sunshine, filled his heart and eyes.

Thus nobly gifted, high-born, opulent, wise,
One hidden curse was his: for troublous years,*
Secretly, swayed in turn by hopes and fears,
And all unknown to her, his heart's desire,
This youth had loved with wild, delirious fire,
The lonely, sad, unconscious Iolene.
He durst not show how love had brought him teen,
Nor prove how deep his passion's inward might;
Thinking, half maddened, on her absent knight;
Save that the burden of a love-lorn lay
Would somewhat of his stifled flame betray,
But in those vague complainings poets use,
When charging Love with outrage and abuse
Of his all-potent witchery. "Ah," said he,
"I love, but ever love despondently;
For though one vision haunts me, and I burn
To hold that dream incarnated, I yearn
In vain, in vain; love breathes no bland return!"

Thus only did Aurelian strive to show
What pangs of hidden passion worked below

---

* We are to suppose that Aurelian had seen Iolene previous to her marriage, and that circumstances had prevented his becoming intimate with her, or in any way prosecuting his suit honestly and frankly.

The surface calmness of his front serene;
Unless perhaps he met his beauteous Queen,
Scarce brightening at the banquet or the dance;
When, with a piercing yet half-piteous glance,
His eyes would search, then strangely shun her face,
As one condemned, who fears to sue for grace.

But on this self-same day, when, homeward bound,
Her footsteps sought the loneliest path that wound
Through tangled copses to the upland ground
And orchard close,—her fair companions kissed
With tearful thanks, and all kind friends dismissed,—
Aurelian, who the secret pathway knew,
Through the dense growth and shrouded foliage drew
Near the pale Queen, the lady of his dreams:
The evening's soft pathetic splendor streams
O'er her clear forehead and her chestnut hair,
All glorified as in celestial air;
But the dark eyes a wistful light confessed,
And some soft murmuring fancies heaved her breast
Benignly, like enamored tides that rise
And sink melodious to the West wind's sighs.
He gazed, and the long passion he had nursed,
Impetuous, sudden, unrestrained, o'erburst
All bounds of custom and enforced restraint:
"O lady, hear me: I am deadly faint,
Yet wild with love! such love as forces man
To beard conventions, trample on the ban
Of partial laws, spurn with contemptuous hate
Whate'er would bar or blight his blissful fate,
And in the feverous frenzy of his zeal,
Even from the shrinking flower he dotes on, steal

Blush, fragrance, and heart-dew! Forgive! forgive!
What! have I dared to tell thee *this*, to live
For aye hereafter in thy cold regard?
Yet veil thy scorn; nor make more cold and hard
The anguished life now cowering at thy feet."

As o'er a billowy field of ripened wheat
One sees perchance the spectral shadows meet,
Cast by a darkened heaven, whose lowering hush
Broods, thunder-charged, above its golden flush,—
So, a dark wonder, a sublime suspense,
Of gathering wrath at this wild insolence,
Dimmed the mild glory of her brow and lips;
Her beauty, more majestic in eclipse,
Shone with that awful lustre which of old,
In the god's temples and the fanes of gold,
Blazed in the Pythia's face, and shook her form
With throes of baleful prophecy; a storm
She stood incarnate, in whose ominous gloom
Throbbed the red lightning on the verge of doom.

But as a current of soft air, unfelt
On the lower earth, is seen ere long to melt
The up-piled surge of tempests slowly driven
In scattered vapors through the deeps of heaven,
Thus a serener thought tenderly played
Across her spirit; its portentous shade,
Big with unuttered wrath and meanings dire,
Began with slow, wan pulsings to expire;
A far ethereal voice she seemed to hear
Luting its merciful accents in her ear,
Subtly harmonious: "Yea," she thought, "in truth,
A rage, a madness holds him, the poor youth

Is drunk with passion! Shall I, deeply blessed
By all love's sweets, its balm and trustful rest,
Crush the less fortunate spirit? utterly
Blight and destroy him, *all for love of me?*
His hopes, if hopes he hath, must surely die;
Still would I nip their blossoms tenderly,
With a slight, airy frost-bite of contempt.
God's mercy, good Sir Squire! art thou exempt
Of courtesy as of reason? What weird spell
Doth work this madness in thee, and compel
Thy nobler nature to such base despites?
Forsooth, thou'lt blush some day the flower of knights,
Should this thy budding virtue wax and grow
To natural consummation! Come! thy flow
Of weak self-ruth might shame the veriest child,
A six years' peevish unchin, whimpering wild,
And scattering his torn locks, because afar
He sees and yearns to clasp, but cannot clasp, a
 star!"

She ceased, with shame and pity weighing down
Her dovelike lids demurely, and a frown
Just struggling faintly with as faint a smile
(For the mute, trembling squire still knelt the while)
Round the arch dimples of her rosy mouth;
Whereon, in fitful fashion, like the South
Which sweeps with petulant wing a field of blooms,
Then dies a heedless death 'mong golden brooms
And lavish shrubbery, briefly she resumes,
With quick-drawn breath, the courses of her speech:
"Aurelian, rise! Behold'st thou yonder beach,
And the blue waves beyond? those bristling rocks,
O'er which the chafed sea, in quick thunder-shocks,

Leaps passionate, panting through the showery spray,
Roaring defiance to the calm-eyed day?
Ah, well, fantastic boy! I blithely swear
When yon rude coast beneath us rises clear
(Down to the farthest bounds of wild Bretaigne),
Of that black rampart darkening sky and main,
I'll pay thy vows with answering vows again,
And be—God save the mark!—thy paramour."

Her words struck keen and deep, even to the core
Of the rash listener's soul; they seemed to be
More fatal in their careless irony
Than if the levin bolt, hurled from above,
Had slain at once his manhood and his love.
What more he felt in sooth 'twere vain to tell;
He only heard her whispering, "Fare-thee-well,
And Heaven assoil thee of all sinful sorrow!"
Then, with a grace and majesty which borrow
Fresh lustrous sweetness from an inward stress
And hidden motion of chaste gentleness,
She glideth like some beauteous cloud apart:
Aurelian saw her pass with yearning pangs at heart.

PART II.

Soul-epochs are there, when Grief's pitiless storm
O'erwhelms the amazèd spirit; when the warm
Exultant heart, whose hopes were brave and high,
Shrinks in the darkness, withering all its sky:
Then, like a wounded bird by the rude wind
Clutched and borne onward, tortured, reckless, blind,
Too frail to struggle with that passionate blast,
We take wild, wavering courses, and at last

Are dashed, it may be, on the rocky verge,
Or hurled o'er the unknown and perilous surge
Of some dark doom, when, bruised and tempest-tost,
We sink in turbulent eddies, and are lost.

Urged by a mood thus desperate, careless what
Thenceforth befell him, from that hateful spot,
The scene of such stern anguish and despair,
Aurelian rushed, he knew not, recked not, where.
All night he wandered in the forest drear,
Till on the pale phantasmal front of morn
The first thin flickering day-gleam glanced forlorn,
Wan as the wraith of perished hopes, the ghost
Of wishes long sustained and fostered most,
Now gone for evermore. "O Christ! that I,"
He muttered hoarsely, "might unsought for lie
Here, in the dismal shadows and dank grass,
And close my heavy eyelids, and so pass
With one brief struggle from the world of men,
Never to grieve or languish,—never again!
Never to sow live seeds of expectation
And joyous promise, to reap desolation;
But as the seasons fly, snow-wreathed, or crowned
With odorous garlands, rest in the mute ground,
Peaceful, oblivious,—a Lethéan cloud
Wrapped round my faded senses like a shroud,
And all earth's turmoil and its juggling show
Dead as a dream dissolved ten thousand years ago!"

Long, long revolving his sad thoughts he stood,
When gleefully from out the lightening wood
Came the sharp ring of horn and echoing steed;
A score of huntsmen, scouring at full speed,

Flashed like a brilliant meteor o'er the scene,
In royal pomp of glimmering gold and green;
Whereat, with wrathful gestures, 'neath the dome
Of the old wood he hastened towards his home,
Where day by day he grew more woeful-pale,
Calling on Heaven unheard to ease his bale.

Among his kinfolk, many in hot haste,
To salve an unknown wound with balms misplaced,
Came the Squire's brother, Curio,—a wise scribe,
Modest withal, and nobler than his tribe;
With heart as loving as his brain was wise:
He could not see with cold, indifferent eyes
Aurelian pass to madness or the grave,
While care and wit of man perchance might save;
So, pondering o'er what seemed a desperate case,
At length there leapt into his kindling face
The flush of a bright thought. "By Heaven!" cried he,
"O brother, there may still be hope for thee;
Therefore, take heart of grace, for what I tell
Doubtless preludes a health-inspiring spell;
And thou, released from this long, sorrowful blight,
Shalt feel the stir of joy, and bless the morning light.

"Ten years—ten centuries sometimes they would seem—
Passed idly o'er me like a mystic's dream;
Ten years agone, when these dull locks of mine
Flowed round broad shoulders with a perfumed shine,
And life's clear glass o'erbrimmed with purpling wine,
I met in Orleans a shrewd clerk-at-law,
One all his comrades loved, yet viewed with awe,

To whom the deepest lore of antique ages,
The storèd secrets of old seers and sages
In Greece, or Ind, or Araby, lay bare:
From out the vacant kingdoms of the air,
He could at will call forth an hundred forms,
Hideous or lovely: the wild wrath of storms;
The zephyr's sweetness; bird, beast, wave, obeyed
The luminous signs his slender wand conveyed,
At whose weird touch men sick in flesh or brain
Became their old, bright, hopeful selves again.
Aurelian, rise! shake off this vile disease,
And ride with me to Orleans; an' it please
God and our Lady, we may chance to meet
Mine ancient comrade, who with deftest feat
Of magic skill may cut the Gordian knot
That long hath bound, and darkly binds thy lot."

"But," said Aurelian, with a listless turn
Of his drooped head, and wandering eyes that burn
With a quick feverish brilliance, "dost thou speak
Of thine own knowledge, when thou bid'st me seek
This rare magician? Hast *thou* looked on aught
Of all the mighty marvels he hath wrought?"

"Yea! I bethink me how, one summer's day,
He led me through the city gates, away
To the dark hollows 'neath a lonely hill:
So hushed the noontide, and so breathless-still
The drowsy air, the voice of one far stream
Came like thin whispers murmuring in a dream;
The blithesome grasshopper, his sense half closed
To all his verdurous luxury, reposed

Pendent upon the quivering, spearlike grain;
Steeped in the mellow sunshine's noiseless rain,
All Nature slept; alone the matron wren,
From the thick coverts of her thorny den,
Teased the hot silence with her twittering low:
My inmost soul accordant, seemed to grow
Languid and dumb within that mystic place.
At length the Wizard's hand across my face
Was waved with gentle motion; a vague mist
Flickered before me, on a sudden kissed
To warmth and glory by an influence bright;
The strangest glamour hovered o'er my sight,
Wherethrough I saw, methought, a palace proud,
Crowned by a lightning-veinèd thunder-cloud,
Whose wreaths of vapory darkness gleamed with eyes
Of multitudinous shifting phantasies;
Its pinnacles like diamond spars outshone
The starry splendors of an Orient zone;
And, leading towards its lordly entrance, rose
Through slow gradations to its marbled close,
White terraces where golden sunflowers bloomed;
Above, a ponderous portal archway loomed,
High-columned, quaint, majestical: we passed
Within that palace, gorgeous, wild, and vast.
Ah, blessed saints! what wonders weirdly blent
Did smite me with a hushed astonishment!
A troop of monsters couchant lined our path,
Their tawny manes and eyes of fiery wrath
Erect and blazing; an unearthly roar
Of fury, shaking vaulted roof and floor,
Burst from each savage, inarticulate throat,
In sullen echoings lost through halls and courts
    remote.

"At the far end of glimmering colonnades
That gleamed gigantic through the dusky shades,
Two mighty doors swept backward noiselessly;
There heaved beyond us a vast laboring sea;
Not vacant, for a stately vessel bore
Swift down the threatening tides that flashed before,
Thronged with black-bearded Titans, such as moved
In far-off times heroic, well-beloved
Of the old gods; there at his stalwart ease,
Shouldering his knotted club, great Hercules
Towered, his fierce eyes touched to dewy light,
And rapt on Hylas, who, serenely bright,
With intense gaze uplifted, tranced and mute,
Heard, in ecstatic reverie, the lute
Of Orpheus plaining to the waves that bow
And dance subsiding round the blazoned prow;
Till the rude winds blew meekly, and caressed
The mimic golden fleeces o'er the crest
Of bard and warrior, on their secret quest
Bound to the groves of Colchis; and the bark,
Round which had frowned a threatening shade and dark,
Now seemed to thrill, like some proud sentient thing
That glories in the prowess of its wing.
The gusty billows of that turbulent sea
Their wild crests smoothed, and slowly, pantingly,
Sunk to the quiet of a charmèd calm;
What odors Hesperéan, what rich balm
Freight the fair zephyrs, as they shyly run
O'er the lulled waters dimpling in the sun!
And murmurings, hark! soft as the long-drawn kiss
Pressed by a young god-lover in his bliss

On lips immortal, when the world was new;
And, lo! across the pure, pellucid blue,
A barge, with silken sails, whose beauteous crew,
Winged Fays and Cupids, curl their sportive arms
O'er one, more lovely in her noontide charms
Than youngest nymphs of Paphos; fragrant showers
Of freshening roses, all luxuriant flowers
That feed on Eastern dews, their fairy bands
Scatter about her from white liberal hands;
While o'er the surface of the dazzling water,
Dark-eyed, mysterious, many an ocean daughter
Flashes a vanishing brightness on her way,
Half seen through tiny twinklings of the spray;
And music its full heart in airy falls
Outpours, like silvery cascades down the walls
Of haunted rocks, and golden cymbals ring,
And lutelike measures on voluptuous wing
Rise gently to the trancèd heavens, replying
From azure-tinted deeps in a low passionate sighing.

"Then were all climes, all ages, wildly blended
On blood-red fields, wherefrom shrill shouts ascended,
Of naked warriors, huge and swart of limb,
Mixed with the mailèd Grecians' ominous hymn,
Where mighty banners starlike waved and shone
'Mid cloven bucklers grandly; and anon
Marched the stern Roman phalanx, with a ring
And clash of spears, and lusty trumpeting,
And steeds that neighed defiance unto death,
And all war's dreadful pomp and hot devouring breath.
Last, on a sudden, the whole tumult died,
The vision disappeared; pale, leaden-eyed,

Bewildered, on the enchanted floor I sank;
When next my wakening spirit faintly drank
Life's consciousness, within my lonely room
I sat, and round me drooped the dreary twilight gloom."

"Enough, good brother! By the Holy Rood
Thy tale is medicinal! the black mood,
Which like a spiritual vulture seized and tore
My heart-strings, and imbued its beak in gore
Hot from the soul, beneath the golden spell
Of sovereign hope hath sought its native hell.
Then, ho! for Orleans!" At the word he sprung
Light to his feet; it seemed there scarcely hung
One trace of his long madness round him now,
So blithe his smile, so bright his kindling brow.
All day they rode till waning afternoon,
Through breezy copses, and the shadowy boon
Of mightier woods, when, as the latest glance
Of sunset, like a level burnished lance,
Smote their steel morions, sauntering near the town,
With thoughtful mien, robed in his scholar's gown,
They met a keen-eyed man, ruddy and tall;
O'er his grave vest a beard of wavy fall
Flowed like a rushing streamlet, rippling down:
"Welcome!" he cried in mellow accents deep;
"The stars have warned me, and my visioned sleep
Foretold your mission, gentles. Curio, what!
Thine ancient, loving comrade quite forgot?
Spur thy dull memory, gossip!"
"By St. Paul!
The learned clerk, the gracious Artevall,
Or glamour's in it," shouted Curio; "yet
Thou look'st as hale, as young, as firmly set

In face and form, as if for thee old Time
Had stopped his flight." A lofty glance, sublime
And swift as lightning, from the Magian's eye
Darted some latent meaning grave and high.
He spake not, but the twain he gently led
Where grassy pathways and fair meads were spread,
Skirting the city walls, till near them stood,
Fronting the gloomy boskage of a wood,
The Wizard's lonely home. I need not pause
To tell how magic and the occult laws
Of sciences long dead that sage's lore
Did in the spectral, midnight hours explore.
Enough, that his strange spells a marvel wrought
Beyond the utmost reach of credulous thought.
At last he said, "Sir Squire, my task is o'er;
Go when thou wilt, and view the Breton shore,
And thou shalt see a wide unwrinkled strand,
Smooth as thy lovely lady's delicate hand,
Washed by a sea o'er which the halcyon West
Broods like a happy heart whose dreams are dreams of
  rest."

PART III.

Meanwhile, Arviragus, a year before
Returned in honor from the English shore,
Led with his faithful Iolene that life
Harmonious, justly balanced, free from strife,
Which crowns our hopes with a true-hearted wife.

Ne'er dreamed he, as she laid her happy head
Close to his heart, what cloud of shame and dread

Gloomed o'er his placid roof-tree; but content
To think how nobly his late toils had spent
Their force beneath Death's gory-dripping brow
Through shocks of battle, a fresh laurel bough
Plucking therefrom, to flourish green and high
About his war-worn temples' majesty,
Gladly from bloodshed, conflicts, and alarms
He rested in those white, encircling arms,
And oft his strong heart thrilled, his eyes grew dim,
To know, kind Heaven! how deep her love for him.

Thus month on month the cheerful days went by,
Like caroling birds across an April sky,
A fairy sky, undimmed by clouds or showers.
But on a morning, while her favorite flowers
Iolene tended, in the garden-walks
Pausing to clip dead leaves, and prop the stalks
Of drooping plants, herself more sweet and fair
Than any flower, the brightest that blushed there,
Her lord stole gently on her unaware;
His haughty grace all softened, he bowed down
To kiss the stray curls of her locks of brown,
Thick-sown with threads of tangled, glimmering
    gold:
"At need," he said, "thou canst be calm and bold;
Therefore, thou wilt not yield to foolish woe
If duty parts us briefly. Wife, I go
To scourge some banded ruffians who of late
Assailed our peaceful serfs, and our estate—
Thou knowest it well—northwest of Penmark town,
Ravished with sword and fire. Thy lord's renown,
Yea, and thy lord, were soon the scoff of all,
If in his own fair fief such crimes befall

Unscourged of justice; so, dear love, adieu!
Nor fear the end of that I have to do."

Thus spake the knight, who forthwith raised a shout,
And bade them bring his stalwart war-horse out;
When, on the sudden, a steed, tall, jet-black,
Led by a groom, came whinnying down the track,
'Twixt the green myrtle hedges; at a bound
He vaulted in the selle; smilingly round
He turned to wave "farewell" with mailèd hand,
And then rode blithely down the sunlit land.

That evening, at the close of vesper-prayer,
Wandering along through the still twilight air,
Iolene, somewhat sad and sick in mind,
Met in her homeward pathway, low-reclined
Beneath the blasted branches of an oak,
Aurelian, her wild lover of old days:
She started backward in a wan amaze.
But he, uprising calmly, bowed and spoke:
"Ha! thou recall'st me, lady? I had deemed
These bitter years which have so scarred and seamed
Whate'er of grace I owned in youthful prime,
Had razed me from thy memory. See! a rime
Like that of age hath touched my locks to white;
Yet never once,—so help me Heaven!—by night
Or day, in storm or brightness, hath my soul
Veered but a point from thee, its starry goal.
A mighty purpose doth itself fulfill,
Wise men have said. Lady! I love thee still,
And Love works marvels. Prithee come with me,
Ay, quickly come, and thou thyself shalt see

I am no falsehood-monger. Yea, come, come!"
His words, his sudden passion, smote her dumb,
And from her cheeks, those delicate gardens, wane
The rare twin roses, as when autumn rain,
Fatally sharp, sweeps o'er some doomed domain
Of matron blooms, and their rich colors fade
Like rainbows slowly dying, shade by shade,
Unto wan spectres of the flowers that were.
With languid head and thoughts of prescient fear,
Passively following where Aurelian guides,
She hears anon the surge and rush of tides
On the seashore, and feels the freshening spray
Bedew her brow. "Lady, look forth, and say
If to a love unquenched, unquenchable,
Eternal Nature yields not; its strong spell
Hath toiled for me, till the rocks rooted under
Those heaving waters have been rent asunder,
And the wide spaces of the ocean plain,
Down to the farthest bounds of wild Bretaigne,
Rise calmly glorious in the day-god's beam.
Look, look thy fill! it is no vanishing dream:
Lo! now I claim thy promise!"
                                    A keen gleam
Shot its victorious radiance o'er his brow.
But she, bewildered, tremulous, shrinking low,
Her clinched hands pale even to the finger-tips,
Pressed on her blinded eyes and faltering lips,
Sued in a voice like wailing wind that breaks
From aspen coverts over lonely lakes,
In the shut heart of immemorial dells,—
A fitful, sobbing voice, whose anguish swells,
Burdened with deep upyearning supplication,
Coldly across his evil exultation.

She pleads for brief delay, with frenzied pain
Grasping at some dim phantom of the brain,
Shadowing a vague deliverance. "As thou wilt,"
He answered, slowly. "Well I know the guilt
Of broken vows can never rest on thee!
Pass by unhurt!" Mutely she turned to flee,
Nor paused until her chambered privacy
She reached with panting sides, pallid as death,
And gasping with short, anguished sobs for breath.
"Caught am I, trapped like a poor fluttering bird,
Or dappled youngling from the innocent herd
Lured to a pitfall! Yet such oath as *this*
Were surely void? If not, he still shall miss—
Whate'er betide—his long-expected bliss!
Better pure-folded arms, and stainless sleep
Where the gray-drooping willow-branches weep,
Than meet a fate so hideous! Let me think!
Others,—pure wives, brave virgins, on the brink
Of shame and ruin, have struck home and fled,
To find unending quiet with the dead."

Borne down as by a demon's hand which pressed
Invisible, but stifling, on her breast,
With brain benumbed, yet burning, and a sense
Of utter, wearied, desperate impotence,—
Her forlorn glance around the darkening room
Roving in helpless search, from out the gloom
Caught the blue glitter of a half-sheathed blade,
A small but trenchant steel, whose lustre played
Balefully bright, and like a serpent's eye
Fixed on her with malign expectancy,
Drew her perforce towards Death,—that death which seemed
The sole, stern means through which her fame, redeemed,

Should soar in spiritual beauty o'er the tomb
Wherein might rest her body's mouldering bloom.

Ah, me! the looks distraught, the passionate care,
The whole wild scene, its misery and despair,
Come back like scenes of yesterday. Half bowed
Her queenly form, and the pent grief allowed
A moment's freedom, shakes her to the core,
The inmost seat of reason. "All is o'er,"
She murmurs, as her slender fingers feel
The deadly edge of the cold shimmering steel.
At once her swift arm flashes to its height,
While the poised death hangs quivering, and her sight
Grows dazed and giddy: when from far, so far
It sounded like the weird voice of a star,
Muffled by distance, yet distinct and deep,
About her in the terrible silence creep
Accents that seize as with a bodily force
On her white arm suspended, and its course
To fatal issues, with arresting will-
Hold rigid, till supine it drops and still,
Back to its drooping level, and a clang
Of the freed steel through all the chamber rang
Sharply, and something shuddered down the air
Like wings of baffled fiends passing in fierce despair.

A warning blent of prescient wrath and prayer
Those accents seemed, wherethrough a palpable dread
Ran coldly shivering. "Pause, pause, pause!" they said;
"Bar not thy hopes 'gainst chance of happier fate!
The circuit vast which rounds life's dial-plate
Hath many lights and shades; its hand which lowers
So threatening *now*, may move to golden hours,

And thou on this sad time may'st look like one
Smiling on mortal woes from some unsetting sun."

Motionless, overcome by hushing awe,
She heard the mystic voice, and dreamed she saw,
Just o'er the dubious borders of the light,
A wavering apparition, scarce more bright
Than one faint moon-ray, through the misty tears
Of clouded evenings seen on breezeless mountain meres.

Mistlike it waned; but in her heart of hearts
The solemn counsel sank: with guilty starts,
She thought how near, through Grief's bewildering
    blight,
How near to death, to death and shame, this night
Her reckless soul had strayed. Yet short-lived hope
Moved hour by hour through paths of narrowing scope,
As, day by day, her term of grace passed by,
Like phantom birds across a phantom sky;
Her lord still absent, and Aurelian bound
(For thus he wrote her) to one weary round,
Morn after morn, of pacings to and fro,
Within the wooded garden-walks below
The city's southward portals. "There," said he,
"Each day, and all day long, impatiently
I wait thy will."

                    As when in dewy spring,
'Mid the moist herbage closely nestling,
Ofttimes we see the hunted partridge cling,
Panting and scared, to the thick-covering grass,
The while above her couch doth darkly pass
What seemeth the shadow of a giant wing,

And she, more lowly, with a cowering stoop,
Shivers, expecting the fell, fiery swoop
Of the gaunt hawk, that corsair of the breeze,
And feels beforehand his sharp talons seize
And rend her tender vitals; so at home,
Iolene, trembling at the stroke to come,
Touched by the lurid shadow of her doom,
Lingered; until, upon a sunny dawn,
Her lord returning, gayly up the lawn
Urged his blithe courser, and, dismounting, came
Upon her, warmly glowing, all aflame
With hope and love. But as her dreary eyes
Were turned on his, a quick, disturbed surprise,
And then a terror, smote him, and the voice
All jubilant, full-breathed to say, "Rejoice,
Our foes are slain!" clave stammering in his throat.
But she, her loose, disheveled locks afloat
Round the fair-sloping shoulders, her hands clasped
About his mailèd knees, brokenly gasped
Her anguish forth, and told her sorrowful tale.
Dizzy and mute, and as the marble pale
Whereon he leaned, unto the desperate close
The knight heard all, locked in a cold repose
More dread than stormiest passion; life and strength
Seemed slowly ebbing from him, till at length
His soul, like one that walks the fatal sand
(Whose treacherous smoothness looks a solid strand,
But tempts to ruin), felt all earth grow dim,
And round him saw, as in a chaos, swim
Joy's fair horizon melting in the cloud.
But soon his stalwart will, rugged and proud,
Woke lionlike to action; a swift flush
Rushed like a sunset river's reddening glow

O'er the tempestuous blackness of his brow,
Pregnant with thunder; through the dismal hush,
His pitiless voice, sharp-echoing round about
The clanging court, leaped like a falchion out.

"Thou hast played with honor as a juggler's ball;
God strikes thee from thy balance, and the thrall
Art thou, henceforth, of one vainglorious deed.
What! shall we plant with rash caprice the seed
Of bitterness, nor look for some harsh fruit
To spring untimely from its poisonous root?
What! a lewd spark, a perfumed popinjay,
Dares in the broad-browed honest gaze of day,
To dash a foul thought, like the hideous spray
Of Hell, right in thy forehead,—and thy hand,
Which should have towered as if the levin-brand
Of scorn and judgment armed it, but a bland
Dismissal signs him! not one hint which tells
Thy lord, meantime, what loathsome secret dwells
Here, by his hearthstone, muffled up, concealed,
And like a corse corrupting, till, revealed
By vengeful doom, its pestilent odor steals
Outward, while all the wholesome blood congeals
To a chill horror, and the air grows vile,
And even the blessed sun a death's-head smile
Assumes in our distempered fantasy?
By Heaven! this withering curse which hangs o'er thee,
O Iolene!"—but here his angry voice
Broke short,—"There is no choice," he moaned, "no choice.
Yea, wife! may Christ adjudge me if I lie,
To endless, as now keen calamity,

But through this troublous gloom my mind discerns
One lonely light to guide us; lo, it burns
Lurid, yet clear, by whose fierce flame I see—
Ah, grief malign! ah, bitter destiny!—
As if God's own right hand the blazing pain
And fiery bale did stamp on soul and brain,
These terms of doom:
>*Shame and despair for both,*
Sorrow and heartbreak! Through all, keep thine oath,
Thou woman, self-involved, self-lost; and so
Face the black front of this tremendous woe!"

She bowed as if a blast of sudden wind,
Breathing full winter, smote her cold and blind;
Then as one wandering in a soul-eclipse,
Feebly she rose, and with her quivering lips
Kissed her pale lord, stifling one desolate cry.
Anon she moved around him noiselessly,
Bent on the small, sweet offices of love;
And sometimes pausing, she would glance above
With tearless eyes, for solemn griefs like this,
Blighting at once both root and flowers of bliss,
Are arid as the desert, and in vain
Thirst for the cooling freshness of the rain.
Fitfully led from treasured nook to nook
Of her dear home, she walked with far-off look,
And absent fingers, plying household tasks;
Bravely her sunless wretchedness she masks
Through moments deemed unending while they passed —
When passed, a flickering point! Hark! The doomed
    hour at last!

   *   *   *   *   *   *   *   *

An afternoon it was, stirless and calm;
From field and garden-close rare breaths of balm
Made the air moist and odorous. Nature lay
Divinely peaceful; only far away
In the broad zenith, a strange cloud unfurled
Its boding banner weirdly o'er the world;
Whilst Iolene, her veiled head sadly bowed,
Passed through the gay thorpe and its motley crowd,
To where a great wall towered this side a wood.
All things her mazed, chaotic fancy viewed
Looked dreamlike; even Aurelian lingering there,
To meet her in the shadiest forest-lair,
Gleamed ghostly dim, a dreadful ghost in sooth,—
For still a hideous trance appeared to press
Upon her, and a nightmare helplessness,—
To whom she knelt in sad mechanic guise,
Pleading for mercy with such piteous eyes,
And such soft flow of self-bewailing ruth,
Aurelian felt his passion's quivering chords
Stilled at the touch of those pathetic words,
That glance of wild, appealing agonies.
Stirred by his nobler nature's grave command
(That fair, indwelling angel sweet and grand,
Born to transmute the worn and blasted soil
Of sinful hearts by his celestial toil
To Eden places and the haunts of God),
He stooped, and, courteous, raised her from the sod,
And whispered closely in her eager ear
Words which his guardian genius smiled to hear;
Words of release, and balmy-breathing cheer.
And while his softening gaze a grateful mist
Feelingly dimmed, with knightly grace he kissed

Her drooping forehead, and loose tressses thrown
In rippling waves adown the heaving zone;
Once, twice, he kissed her thus, with reverence meek;
But when her brimming eyes uplifted, seek
Aurelian now, with eloquent looks to tell
What tenderest words could not convey so well,
She only sees the tree-stems tall and brown,
The golden leaves come faintly fluttering down,
And only hears the wind of sunset moan:
Midmost the twilight wood the lady stands alone.

Stung by his misery into frenzied motion,
Her lord meantime beside the restless ocean
Roamed, hearkening to the mournful undertone
Of the sea's mighty heart, which touched his own,
O God, how sadly! when abruptly lifting
His furrowed brow long fixed upon the shifting
And mimic whirlwinds of loose sand that flew
Hither and thither, as the brief winds blew
At fitful whiles from o'er the watery waste,
He saw, as if she spurned the earth in haste,
His gentle wife returning, with a face
Whereon there dwelt no shadow of disgrace;
A face that seemed transfigured in the light
Of Paradise, it shone so softly bright.
Beautiful ever, round her now there hovered
A subtle, new-born glory, which discovered
A shape so dazzling, you had thought the plume
Of some archangel's pinion cast its bloom
About her, and the veil of heaven withdrawn,
She viewed the mystic streams, the sapphire dawn,
And heard the choirs celestial, tier on tier
Uptowering to the uttermost golden sphere,

Sing of a vanquished dread, a blest release,
The effluence and the solemn charm of peace.

Evening closed round them; o'er the placid reach
Stretching far northward of the sea-girt beach,
They passed, while night's first planet in the sky
Faltered from out the stillness timidly,
And perfumed breezes rustled murmuring by,
'Twixt the grim headlands up the glens to die,
And white-winged sea-birds, with a long-drawn cry
Which spake of homeward flight and billowy nest,
Glanced through the sunset down the wavering West.

Evening closed o'er them, mellowing into dark;
Along the horizon's edge, a tiny spark,
Dull-red at first, but broadening to a white
And tranquil orb of silvery-streaming light,
Slowly the Night Queen fair her heaven ascends:
The outlines of those loving forms she blends
Into one luminous shade, which seems to float,
Mingle and melt in shining mists remote;
Type of two perfect lives whose single soul
Outbreathes a cordial music, sweet and whole,
One will, one mind, one joy-encircled fate,
And one winged faith that soars beyond the heavenly
    gate.

My song which now hath long flowed unperplexed
Through scenes so various, calm as heaven, or vexed
By gusty passion, reaches the lone shore,
Ghostlike and strange, of silence and old dreams;
Far-off its weird and wandering whisper seems
Like airs that faint o'er untracked oceans hoar

On haunted midnights, when the moon is low.
And now 'tis ended: long, yea, long ago,
Lost on the wings of all the winds that blow,
The dust of these dead loves hath passed away;
Still, still, methinks, a soft ethereal ray
Illumes the tender record, and makes bright
Its heart-deep pathos with a marvelous light,
So that whate'er of frenzied grief and pain
Marred the pure currents of the crystal strain,
Transfigured shines through fancy's mellowing trance,
Touching with golden haze the quaint old-world romance.

NOTE.—Of "The Frankleines Tale," the plot of which has been followed in "The Wife of Brittany," Richard Henry Horne, the author of "Orion," says: "It is a noble story, perfect in its moral purpose, and chivalrous self-devotion to a feeling of truth and honor; but it would have been more satisfactory in an intellectual sense had a distinction been made between a sincere pledge of faith and a 'merry bond'!"

This may at first seem incontrovertible, but we should remember that Chaucer, who, without pretension, and through the medium of his humor, satire, and pathos, was the great moralist and preacher of his time, desired in "The Frankleines Tale" to show the danger of too lightly treating, from whatever motive, such solemn obligations as those connected with a wife's chastity and honor.

Moreover, in the mediæval age, a superstitious sanctity was often made to attach to one's word, no matter how unthinkingly it may have been given; nay, it was maintained by certain strict formalists, that even an *extorted* oath was, under some conditions, binding! It will, therefore, be perceived, that in allowing so much importance to a "merry bond," and associating with it such grave trials, the poet was true both to the time depicted and to human nature, as influenced by morbid and conventional ideas of duty.

THE RIVER.

["Man's life is like a River, which likewise hath its Seasons or phases of progress: first, its Spring rise, gentle and beautiful; next, its Summer, of eventful maturity, mixed calm, and storm, followed by Autumnal decadence, and mists of Winter, after which cometh the all-embracing Sea, type of that mystery we call Eternity!"]

Up among the dew-lit fallows
   Slight but fair it took its rise,
And through rounds of golden shallows
   Brightened under broadening skies;
While the delicate wind of morning
   Touched the waves to happier grace,
Like a breath of love's forewarning,
   Dimpling o'er a virgin face,—
Till the tides of that rare river
   Merged and mellowed into one,
Flashed the shafts from sundawn's quiver,
   Backward to the sun.

Royal breadths of sky-born blushes
   Burned athwart its billowy breast,—
But beyond those roseate flushes
   Shone the snow-white swans at rest;
Round in graceful flights the swallows
   Dipped and soared, and soaring sang,
And in bays and reed-bound hollows,
   How earth's wild, sweet voices rang!
Till the strong, swift, glorious river
   Seemed with mightier pulse to run,
Thus to roll and rush forever,
   Laughing in the sun.

Nay; a something born of shadow
　　Slowly crept the landscape o'er,—
Something weird o'er wave and meadow,
　　Something cold o'er stream and shore;
While on birds that gleamed or chanted,
　　Stole gray gloom and silence grim,
And the troubled wave-heart panted,
　　And the smiling heavens waxed dim,
And from far strange spaces seaward,
　　Out of dreamy cloud-lands dun,
Came a low gust moaning leaward,
　　Chilling leaf and sun.

Then, from gloom to gloom intenser,
　　On the laboring streamlet rolled,
Where from cloud-racks gathered denser,
　　Hark! the ominous thunder knolled!
While like ghosts that flit and shiver,
　　Down the mists, from out the blast,
Spectral pinions crossed the river,—
　　Spectral voices wailing passed!
Till the fierce tides, rising starkly,
　　Blended, towering into one
Mighty wall of blackness, darkly
　　Quenching sky and sun!

Thence, to softer scenes it wandered,
　　Scents of flowers and airs of balm,
And methought the streamlet pondered,
　　Conscious of the blissful calm;
Slow it wound now, slow and slower
　　By still beach and ripply bight,
And the voice of waves sank lower,
　　Laden, languid with delight;

In and out the cordial river
   Strayed in peaceful curves that won
Glory from the great Life-Giver,
   Beauty from the sun!

Thence again with quaintest ranges,
   On the fateful streamlet rolled
Through unnumbered, nameless changes,
   Shade and sunshine, gloom and gold,
Till the tides, grown sad and weary,
   Longed to meet the mightier main,
And their low-toned *miserere*
   Mingled with his grand refrain;
Oh, the languid, lapsing river,
   Weak of pulse and soft of tune,—
Lo! the *sun* hath set forever,
   Lo! the ghostly moon!

But thenceforth through moon and starlight
   Sudden-swift the streamlet's sweep;
Yearning for the mystic far-light,
   Pining for the solemn deep;
While the old strength gathers o'er it,
   While the old voice rings sublime,
And in pallid mist before it,
   Fade the phantom shows of time,—
Till with one last eddying quiver,
   All its checkered journey done,
Seaward breaks the ransomed river,
   Goal and grave are won!

THE NEST.

4-24-'85.

At the poet's life-core lying
  Is a sheltered and sacred nest,
Where, as yet, unfledged for flying,
  His callow fancies rest:

Fancies, and Thoughts, and Feelings,
  Which the mother Psyche breeds,
And Passions whose dim revealings
  But torture their hungry needs.

Yet,—there cometh a summer splendor
  When the golden brood wax strong,
And, with voices grand or tender,
  They rise to the heaven of song.

THE LITTLE SAINT.

At the calm matin hour
  I see her bend in prayer,
As bends a virgin flower
  Kissed by the summer air:
O! meek her downcast eyes!
  But the sweet lips wear a smile;
How hard the little angel tries
  To be serious all the while!

I tell her 'tis not right
   To be half grave, half gay,
Imploring in Heaven's sight
   A blessing on the day:
She hears, and looks devout
   (Although it gives her pain);
Still, when the ritual's almost out,
   She's sure to smile again!

She shocks her maiden aunt,
   Who thinks it a disgrace
That—do her best—she can't
   Give her a solemn face:
She'll scold, and rate, and fume,
   And lecture hour by hour,
Until she makes the *very room*
   Look passionate and sour!

Alack! 'tis all in vain!
   Soon as the sermon's done,
My fairy blooms again,
   Like a rosebud in the sun;
I cannot damp her mirth,
   I will not check her play,—
Is innocent joy so rife on earth
   Hers should not have full sway?

I asked her yester-night,
   Why, when prayer was made,
Her brow of cordial light
   Scarce caught one serious shade.
"Father," she said, "*you* love
   Better to meet me glad,
And so, I thought, the Christ above
   Might grieve to see me sad!"

THE STORY OF GLAUCUS THE THESSALIAN.*

TO ———.

List to this legend, which an antique poet
Hath left among the musty tomes of eld,
Like a flushed rosebud pressed between the leaves
Of some worn, dark-hued volume. What a light
Of healthful bloom about it! What an air
Seems breathing round its delicate petals still!
Wilt thou not take it, lady,—thou, whose face
Is lovely as a lost Arcadian dream,—
And place it next thy heart, and keep it fresh
With balmy dews thy gentle spirit sends
Up to the deep founts of the tenderest eyes
That e'er have shone, I think, since in some dell
Of Argos and enchanted Thessaly,
The poet, from whose heart-lit brain it came,
Murmured this record unto her he loved?

THE STORY.

Glaucus, a young Thessalian, while the dawn
Of a fresh spring-tide brightened copse and lawn,
Sauntered, with lingering steps and dreamy mood,
Adown the fragrant pathway of a wood
Which skirted his small homestead pleasantly,—
And there he saw a tall, majestic tree,

---

* The elements of this story are to be found in Apollonius Rhodius, and Leigh Hunt has embodied them in a graceful prose legend.

An oak of untold summers, whose broad crown,
Quivering as if in some slow agony,
And trembling inch by inch forlornly down,
Threatened, for want of a kind propping care,
To leave its breezy realm of golden air,
And from its leafy heights, with shriek and groan,
Like some proud forest empire overthrown,
Measure its vast bulk on the greensward lone.

Glaucus beheld and pitied it. He saw
The approaching ruin with a touch of awe,
No less than genial sympathy,—for men,
In those old times, pierced with a wiser ken
To the deep soul of Nature, and from thence
Drew a serene and mystic influence,
Which thrilled all life to music. Therefore he
Called on his slaves, and bade them prop the tree.
Musing he passed to a still lonelier place
In the dim forest, by this act of grace
Lightened and cheered, when, from the copse-wood
    nigh,
There dawned upon his vision suddenly
A shape more fair and lustrous than the star
Which rides o'er Cloudland on her sapphire car
When vesper winds are fluting solemnly.
"Glaucus," she said, in tones whose liquid flow,
Mellow, harmonious, passionately low,
Stole o'er his spirit with a strange, wild thrill,
"I am the Nymph of that fair tree thy will
Hath saved from ruin; but for thee my breath
Had vanished mistlike,—my glad eyes in death
Been sealed for evermore. Yes! but for thee
I must have lost that half-divinity

Whose secret essence, spiritually fine,
Hath warmed my veins like Hebe's heavenly wine.
No more, no more amid my rippling hair
Could I have felt soft fingers of the Air
Dallying at dawn or twilight,—on my cheek
Have felt the sun rest with a rosy-streak,
Pulsing in languor; nor with pleasant pain
Drooped in the cool arms of the loving Rain,
That wept its soul out on my bosom fair.
But now, in long, calm, blissful days to be,
This life of mine shall lapse deliciously
Through all the seasons of the bounteous year;
Beneath my shade mortals shall sit, and hear
Benignant whispers in the shimmering leaves;
And sometimes, upon warm and odorous eves,
Lovers shall bring me offerings of sweet things,—
Honey and fruit,—and dream they mark the wings
Of Cupids fluttering through the oak-boughs hoar.
All this I owe thee, Glaucus,—all, and more!
Ask what thou wilt!—thou shalt not ask in vain!"

Then Glaucus, gazing in her glorious eyes,
And rallying from his first unmanned surprise,
Emboldened, too, by her soft looks, which drew
A spell about his heart like fire and dew
Mingled and melting in a love-charm bland,—
And by the twinkling of her moon-white hand,
That seemed to beckon coyly to her side,
And by her maiden sweetness deified,
And something that he deemed a dear unrest
Heaving the unveiled billows of her breast—
(As if her preternatural part, as free
And wild as any nursling of the lea,

Yearned wholly downward to humanity)—
Emboldened thus, I say, Glaucus replied:
"O fairest vision! be my love,—my bride!"

Over her face there passed an airy flush,
The roseate shade, the twilight of a blush,
Ere the low-whispering answer pensively
Stirred the dim silence in its trancèd hush.
"Thy suit is granted, Glaucus! though perchance
A peril broods o'er this, thy bright romance,
Like a lone cloudlet o'er a lake that's fair.
When the high noon, flaunting so hotly now
Fades into evening, thou may'st meet me here,
Just in the cool of this rill-shadowing bough;
My favorite Bee, my fairy of the flowers,
Shall bid thee come to that pure tryst of ours."

Who now so proud as Glaucus? "I have won,"
Lightly he said, "the marvelous benison
Of love from her in whose soft-folding arms
Gods might forget Elysium! O! her charms
Are perfect,—perfect heaven and perfect earth,
Blest and commingled in one exquisite birth
Of beauty,—and for me! I know not why,
But rosy Eros ever seems to fly
Gayly before me, armed for victory,
In every pleasant love-strife!" On this theme
Deeply he dwelt, till a vain self-esteem
Obscured his worthier spirit. Thus he went
Out from the haunted wood, his nature toned
Down to the common daylight, disenzoned
Of all its rare, ethereal ravishment.

Still in this mood, he sought the neighboring town,
Met with some gay young comrades, and sat down
To dice and wassail. All that morn he played,
And quaffed, and sang, and feasted, till the shade
Of evening o'er earth's forehead cast a gloom;
And still he played, when on his ear the boom
Of a swift, shining, yellow-breasted Bee
Rung out its small alarum. Teasingly
The insect hummed about him, went and came,
And like a tiny hell of circling flame
And discord seemed to Glaucus, who at last
Struck at the wingèd torment testily.
The Bee—poor go-between!—in either thigh
Cruelly maimed, with feeble flutterings, passed
Back to its home amid the foliaged bloom.

At length, in two most fortunate throws, the game
Was won by Glaucus! With triumphant smile
He seized and pocketed a glittering pile
Of new sestertii. "Ay! 'tis e'er the same,"
He muttered; "dice or women, I *must* win!
But hold!—by Venus! 'twere a burning sin,
And false to my fond wild flower of the wood
Longer to dally here. O Fortune! good,
Kind mistress, speed me still! Would that each heel
Were plumed like happy Hermes'!" His late zeal
Spurred the youth onward to the place of tryst,—
One final burst of sunset—amethyst,
Ruby, and topaz—blazed among the boughs,
Whence a sad voice,—"*Breaker of solemn vows,
What dost thou here? Thine hour has past for aye!*"
Glaucus, with startled eyes, peered through the sway
Of moistened fern and thicket, but his view

Rested alone on vacancy, or caught,
Swift as the shifting glamour of a thought,
Only the golden and evanishing ray,
Which, softened by cool sparkles of the dew,
Flashed through the half-closed lids of weary Day.

"Here am I," said the voice, so sadly sweet,
The listener thrilled even to his pausing feet,—
"Here, right before thee, Glaucus!"   Yet again
The youth, with straining eyeballs and hot brain,
Searched the dense thickets,—it was all in vain.
"Alas! alas!" (and now a tremulous moan
Sobbed through the voice, like a faint minor tone
In mournful human music)—"thou canst see
My face no more, for sternly, drearily,
A wildering cloud of sense, that shall not rise,
Hath come between me and thy darkening eyes.
O shallow-hearted! nevermore on thee
Shall visions of that finer world above
Dawn from the chaste auroras of their love;
But common things, seen in a funeral haze
Of earthiness, and sorrow, and mistrust,
Weigh the soul down, and soil its hopes with dust;
A hand like Fate's with cruel force shall press
Thy spirit backward into heaviness,
And the base realm of that forlorn abyss
Wherein the serpent Passions writhe and hiss
In savage desolation!   Blind, blind, blind
Art thou henceforth in heart, and hope, and mind!
For he to whom my messenger of joy
And soothing promise only brought annoy
And sharp disquiet in his low-born lust,—
What, what to him *Ideal Beauty's* kiss,

The charm of lofty converse in the dells,
Of divine meetings, musical farewells,
And glimpses through the flickering leaves at night
Of such fair mysteries in awe-hushing light
That even I, who in these forests dwell
Purely with innocent creatures, unto whom
All Nature opes her innermost heart of bloom
And blessedness, by some majestic spell
Uplifted unto realms ineffable,
Faint almost in the splendor large and clear?
The winds have ceased their murmurings,—on my ear
The rill-songs melt to threads of delicate tune,
And every small mote dancing in the moon
Expands, and brightens to a spiritual eye,
Luring me up to Immortality.
O! then my earthly nature, loosening, slips
Down like a garment, and invisible lips
Whisper the secrets of their happier sphere!
This bliss, O youth! my soul had shared with one
Worthy the gift! Alas! *thou* art not he!"

The voice died off toward the waning sun!
Glaucus looked up,—the gaunt, gray forest trees
Seemed to close o'er him like a vault of stone.
"*Just Gods!*" he sighed, "*I am indeed alone!*"

SONNET.

Hast thou beheld a landscape dull and bare,
  On which, at times, a flying gleam was shed
  From some shy sunbeam shifting overhead,
That made the scene for one brief moment fair?
Such is the light, so transient, flickering, rare,
  Which, from Fate's sullen heavens above me spread,
  Hath flushed the path my weary footsteps tread,
And lent to Darkness glimpses of sweet cheer.
Alas! alas! that I, whose soul doth burn
  With such deep passion for a steadfast bliss,
Must bend forever o'er Hope's burial urn,
  And greet even Love with a half-mournful kiss!
  In sooth, what stern, malignant doom is this?
Joy! delicate Ariel! ah! return! return!

MARGUERITE.

She was a child of gentlest air,
Of deep-dark eyes, but golden hair,
And, ah! I loved her unaware,
          Marguerite!

She spelled me with those midnight eyes,
The sweetness of her naïve replies,
And all her innocent sorceries,
          Marguerite!

The fever of my soul grew calm
Beneath her smile that healed like balm,
Her words were holier than a psalm,
   Marguerite!

But 'twixt us yawned a gulf of fate,
Whose blackness I beheld,—too late.
O Christ! that LOVE *should smite like* HATE,
   Marguerite!

She did not wither to the tomb,
But round her crept a tender gloom
More touching than her earliest bloom,
   Marguerite!

The sun of one fair hope had set,
A hope she dared not all forget,
Its twilight glory kissed her yet,—
   Marguerite!

And ever in that twilight fair
Moves with deep eyes and golden hair
The child who loved ME unaware!
   Marguerite!

NOT DEAD.

TO J. A. D.

HERE, at the sweetest hour of this sweet day,—
    Here, in the calmest woodland haunt I know,—
Benignant thoughts around thy memory play,
    And in my heart do pleasant fancies blow,
    Like flowers turned to thee, radiant and aglow,
Flushed by the light of times forever fled,
Whose tender glory pales, but is not dead.

The warm South-wind is like thy generous breath,
    Laden with kindly words of gentle cheer,
And every whispering leaf above me saith,
    She whom thou dream'st so distant hovers near;
    Her love it is that thrills the sunset air
With mystic motions from a time that's fled,—
Long past and gone, in sooth,—but, oh! not dead!

The drowsy murmur of cool brooks below;
    The soft, slow clouds that seem to *muse* on high;
Love-notes of hidden birds, that come and go,
    Making a sentient Rapture of the sky;
    All the rare season's peaceful sorcery,
These hint of cordial joys, forever fled,—
Joys past, indeed, and yet they are not dead:

Far from the motley throng of sordid men,
    From fashion far, mean strife, and frenzied gain,

NOT DEAD.

In those dear days through many a mountain glen,
   By mountain streams, and fields of rippling grain,
   We roamed, untouched by Passion's feverish pain,
But quaffing Friendship's tranquil draughts instead,—
Its waters clear whose sweetness is not dead!

Above that nook of fair remembrance stands
   A dove-eyed Faith, that falters not, nor sleeps;
No flowers of Lethe droop in her white hands,
   And if the watch that steadfast angel keeps
   Be pensive, and some transient tears she weeps,
They are but tears a fond regret may shed
O'er twilight joys which fade, but are not dead!

Not dead! not dead! but glorified and fair,
   Like yonder marvelous cloudland floating far
Between the mellowing sunset's amber air
   And the mild lustre of eve's earliest star,—
   Oh, such, so pure, so bright, these memories are!
Earth's warmth and Heaven's serene around them spread,—
They pass, they wane, but, Sweet! they are not dead!

APART.

Come not with empty words that say,
"Your strength of manhood wastes away
In long, ignoble, fruitless years!"
I live apart from pain and tears,
Wherewith the ways of men are sown,—
Nor dwell I loveless, and alone;
One tender spirit shares my days,
One voice is swift to yield me praise,
One true heart beats against my own!
What more, what more could man desire
Than love that burns a steadfast fire,
And faith that ever leads him higher
Along the paths which point to peace?

Oh, far and faint I hear the din
Of battle-blows, and mortal sin
From out the stir and press of life;
Those hollow, muffled sounds of strife
Seem rolled from thunder-clouds upcurled
About a dim and distant world,
Below me, in the sunless gloom;
But round my brow the amaranths bloom
Of sober joy with heart's-ease furled;
For more, what more can man desire
Than love that burns a steadfast fire,
And faith that ever leads him higher,
Where all the jars of earth shall cease?

A present glory haunts my way,
A promise of diviner day
Illumes the flushed horizon's verge;
And fainter, farther still, the surge
Of buffeting waves that beat and roar
Up the dim world's tempestuous shore
Beneath me in the moonless airs;
Alas, its passions, sorrows, cares!
Alas, its fathomless despairs!
Yet dreams, vague dreams, they seem to me,
On these clear heights of liberty,
These summits of serene desire,—
Whence love ascends, a quenchless fire,
And sweet faith ever leads me higher
To pearly paths of perfect peace!

"IN UTROQUE FIDELIS."

Along the woods the whispering night-airs swoon,
    A single bird-note dies adown the trees,
Clear, pallid, mournful, droops the summer moon,
    Dipped in the foam of cloudland's phantom seas;—
        Soundless they heave above
The dim, ancestral home that holds my love.

How breathless-still! A mystic glamour keeps
    Calm watch and ward o'er this weird, drowsy hour:
Yon heaven's at peace, the earth benignly sleeps;
    And thou, thou slumberest too, my woodland flower,—
        Fair lily steeped in light
And happy visions of the marvelous night!

I waft a sigh from this fond soul to thine,—
    A little sigh, yet honey-laden, dear,
With fairy freightage of such hopes divine
    As fain would flutter gently at thine ear,
        And, entering, find their way
Down to the heart so veiled from me by day.

In dreams, in dreams, perchance, thou art not coy;
    And one keen hope more bold than all the rest
May touch thy spirit with a tremulous joy,
    And stir an answering softness in thy breast:
        O sleep! O blest eclipse!
What murmured word is faltering at her lips?

Awake for one brief moment, genial South:
    Breathe o'er her slumbers,—waft that word to me,
Warm with the fragrance of her rosebud mouth,
    Enwreathed in smiles of dreamful fantasy:
        Come, whisper, low and light,
The name which haunts her maiden trance to-night.

Still, breathless-still! No voice in earth or air:
    I only know my delicate darling lies,
A twilight lustre glimmering in her hair,
    And dews of peace within her languid eyes:
        Yea, only know that I
Am called from love and dreams, perhaps to die,—

Die when the heavens are thick with scarlet rain,
    And every time-throb's fated: even there
Her face would shine through mists of mortal pain,
    And sweeten death, like some incarnate prayer:
        Hark! 'tis the trumpet's swell!
O love! O dreams! farewell, farewell, farewell!

THE LOTOS AND THE LILY.

The little poems which follow were suggested by an Oriental idea developed in Alger's "Specimens of Eastern Poetry." The MOON is strangely spoken of as masculine.

THE LOTOS.

DROOPING in the sunlit streams,
We are wrapped all day in dreams;

Morn and noon and evening light
Robed for us in garbs of night.

Only when the moon appears
Through a silvery mist of tears,

From the waters dark and still,
We arise to drink our fill

Of the tender love he sheds
On our fair enamored heads.

Ah! no longer wrapped in dreams,
How we pant beneath his beams!

How, with breath of softest sighs,
We unclose our yearning eyes,

And our snowy necks in pride
Curve about the glittering tide!

Warmth for warmth and kiss for kiss,
All our pulses burn with bliss,

Till revealed our inmost charms
Glowing in the Night-God's arms.

THE LILY.

View us, white-robed Lilies,
   We whose beauty's rareness
Sleeps until the Bridegroom Sun
   Woos our virgin fairness.

Then, our bosoms baring,
   'Neath his ardent kisses,
Stem, and leaf, and delicate heart
   Trembling into blisses,

The full, fervid Godhead
   Thrills our being tender,
And our happy souls expand
   In ecstatic splendor.

Thus all, *all* we yield him
   Of our shrinèd sweetness,—
All that maiden warmth may grant
   To true love's completeness.

WINDLESS RAIN.

THE rain, the desolate rain!
  Ceaseless, and solemn, and chill!
How it drips on the misty pane,
  How it drenches the darkened sill!
O scene of sorrow and dearth!
  I would that the wind awaking
To a fierce and gusty birth
    Might vary this dull refrain
    Of the rain, the desolate rain:
  For the heart of heaven seems breaking
In tears o'er the fallen earth,
  And again, again, again
  We list to the sombre strain,
The faint, cold, monotone—
Whose soul is a mystic moan—
Of the rain, the mournful rain,
The soft, despairing rain!

The rain, the murmurous rain!
  Weary, passionless, slow,
'Tis the rhythm of settled sorrow,
  'Tis the sobbing of cureless woe!
And all the tragic of life,
  The pathos of Long-Ago,
    Comes back on the sad refrain
    Of the rain, the dreary rain,
Till the graves in my heart unclose,
  And the dead who are buried there

From a solemn and weird repose
   Awake,—but with eyeballs drear,
And voices that melt in pain
On the tide of the plaintive rain,
The yearning, hopeless rain,
The long, low, whispering rain!

CHLORIS.

WHAT time the rosy-flushing West
   Sleeps soft on copse and dingle,
Wherein the sunset shadows rest,
   Or richly float and mingle;

When down the vale the wood-dove's note
   Thrills in a cadence tender,
And every rare, ethereal mote
   Turns to a wingèd splendor;

Just as the mystic cloudlands ope,
   Far up their sapphire portal,
Fair as the fairest dream of Hope,
   Half goddess and half mortal,—

I see that lovely Genius rise,
   That child of Orient trances,
On whose sweet face the glory lies
   Of weird Hellenic fancies,—

CHLORIS! beneath whose procreant tread
  All earth yields up her sweetness,—
The violet's scent, the rose's red,
  The dahlia's orbed completeness,—

And verdures on the myriad hills,
  The breath of her pure duty
Hath nursed to life by sparkling rills
  And foliaged nooks of beauty;

Till bloom and odor, blush and song,
  So fill earth's radiant spaces,—
The fading touch of sin, or wrong,
  Leaves glad the weariest faces;

And so, through happy spring-tide dells,
  O'er mount, and field, and river,
Her Zephyr's fairy clarion swells,
  Her footsteps glance forever!

NATURE, BETROTHED AND WEDDED.

HAVE you not noted how in early Spring,
From out the forests, past the murmuring brooks,
O'er the hillsides, Nature, with airy grace,
Like some fair virgin, touched by lights and shades,
Glides timidly, a veil of golden mist
About her brows, and budding bosom draped
In maiden coyness? She's a Bride betrothed

Unto that mystic god, who comes from far,
Rich Orient lands upon the winds of June,
That bear him like swift Ardours, winged with fire;
And when, on some calm, lustrous morn, her Lord
Uplifts the golden veil, and weds to hers
The quickening warmth of ripe, immortal lips,
How the broad Earth leaps into raptured life,
And thrills with music!

                Then, a queenly spouse,
Raised unto fruitful empire, through all hours
Of bounteous Summer, she walks proudly on,
Shining with blissful eyes of matronhood,
Till, at the last, Autumn, with reverent hand,
Doth crown her with such full, completed joy,
Such wealth of sovereign beauty, she once more
About her brows and sumptuous bosom folds
That golden veil,—not in the tremulous fear
Of maiden coyness *now*, but lest rash men,
Drawn by her awful loveliness, should dare
To gaze too closely on it, and thus fall,
Smitten and blind, at her imperial feet!

FORTUNIO.

A PARABLE FOR THE TIMES.

Who at the court of Astolf, the great King,
King of a realm of firs, and icy floes,
Cold bright fiords, and mountains capped with clouds,—
Who there so loved and honored as the knight,
The youthful knight, Fortunio? Whence he came,
None knew, nor whom his kindred: at a bound
He passed all rivals moving towards the throne,
And stood firm-poised above them; yet with mien
So sweet, it honeyed envy, and surprised
The bitterest railers into complaisance!
Low-voiced and delicate-featured, with a check
As soft as peach down, or the golden dust
Shrined in a maiden lily's heart of hearts,—
Yet a stern will bent bowlike, with the shaft
Of some keen purpose swiftly drawn to head,
Or launched unerring at its lofty mark,—
Rose thrilled with action, or high-strung at aim,
Beneath his jeweled doublet! While the hand
So warm, so white, and wont to press the palm
In palpitating clasp of fair sixteen,
Could wield the ponderous battle-axe, or flash
The lightning rapier in a foeman's eyes.
Prince of the tourney and the dance alike,
War's fiercer lists had seen his furrowless brow
Flushed red with heat of battle, heard his voice
Shrilled clear beyond the clarions, mount and break

In larklike song far o'er the mists of blood,
Through Victory's calmer heaven. Mixed love and fear,
With love ofttimes preponderant, girded him
Closely, as with an atmosphere disturbed
Only by hints of thunder, ghosts of cloud.
But love, all love, love in her passionate eyes,
Love 'twixt the pure twin rosebuds of her mouth,
Love in the arch of brooding, beauteous brows,
And every wavering dimple wherein smiles
At hide-and-seek with sly, mock frownings played,—
All love was Freyla, though a princess she,
For this unknown Fortunio! Wildly beat
And burned her heart at each soft glance he gave,
Or softer word, albeit as yet unthrilled
By answering passion! Swiftly flew her dreams
Birdlike on balmy winds of fancy borne,
To bridal realms empurpled and divine,—
Alas! but Scorn, that long had lurked and spied
In ambush, shot its sudden bolts, and brought
Those wingèd Dreams transfixed to earth and dead!
While Rage, Scorn's ally, in her father's breast,
Clutched the sweet dreamer rudely, dragged her soul
Into the garish glare of Commonplace
(Soon to be lit by Horror's lurid star!)
And so convulsed her tenderness with threats,
That all her being seemed collapsed to fall
Crushed, as in moral earthquake: "Doting fool,"
Outshrieked the King, "dost dream great Odin's blood
Could mix with veins plebeian? Purge thy thoughts,
Unvirgined, vile, of sacrilegious sin!
But for this boy, our twelvemonth's grace hath raised
So high, a moment's justice shall cast down
To fathomless depths of ruin!"

                                    Wherewithal
(Harping on justice still, though justice slept)
The King decreed, "This youth Fortunio dies!"
So, on a bright spring morn, the knight stood up,
Fronting the royal doomsmen, with a face
Sublimely calm; they tore his bravery off,
His jeweled vest and knighthood's golden spurs,
And bared his heart to catch the arrowy hail,—
When lo! beneath those rough, disrobing hands,
*The dangerous, lewd seducer, coyly bowed,
Outbeamed a virgin beauty chaste and fair!*

The King, beholding, started, and then smiled:
"Thou wanton madcap," said he, "go in peace!"

O cordial eyes, the brown eyes and the blue,
Or ye dark eyes, with deeps like midnight heavens,
Where unimagined worlds of thought and love
Shine starlike, would ye quench your glorious rays
In the low levels of the lives of men?
O gracious souls of women tender-sweet,
And luminous with goodness, would ye soil
Your nascent angel-plumage in the sty
Of sordid worldliness? Be warned, be warned!
Set not the frail spears of your rash caprice
In rest against great Nature's pierceless shield;
Strive not to grasp monopolies impure,
Man's fated heritage. Be warned, be warned!
For surely as yon bright sun dawns and dies,
And sure as Nature, all immutable,
Year after year completes her mystic round
Through law's vast orbit,—so ye desperate Fair,
Arrayed against the eternal force of God,

Must fall discomfited, and like that knight,
The false Fortunio, rest your claims at last,
Not on deft spells of simulated power,
But on the soft white bosom which enspheres
The sacred charms of perfect womanhood!

STONEWALL JACKSON.

I.

THE fashions and the forms of men decay,
The seasons perish, the calm sunsets die,
Ne'er with the *same* bright pomp of cloud or ray
To flush the golden pathways of the Sky;
All things are lost in dread Eternity,—
States, Empires, Creeds, the Lay
Of master Poets, even the shapes of Love,
Bear ever with them an invisible Shade,
Whose name is death; we cannot breathe nor move,
But that we touch the Darkness, till dismayed,
We feel the imperious Shadow freeze our hearts,
And mortal Hope grows pale and fluttering Life departs.

II.

All things are lost in dread Eternity,
Save that majestic VIRTUE which is given
Once, twice, perchance beneath our earthly Heaven,
To some great Soul in ages: O! the Lie,
The base, incarnate Lie we call the World,
Shakes at his coming, as the forest shakes,
When mountain storms with bannered clouds unfurled,

Rush down and rend it; sleek Convention drops
Its glittering mass, and hoary, cobwebbed rules
Of petty Charlatans or insolent fools
Shrink to annihilation,—Truth awakes,
A morning splendor in her fearless eyes
    Touching the delicate stops
Of some rare Lute which breathes of promise fair,
    Or pouring on the covenanted air
A trumpet blast which startles, but makes strong,
    While ancient Wrong,
Driven like a beast from his deep-caverned lair,
    Grows gaunt, and inly quakes,
Knowing that Retribution draws so near!

III.

    Whether with Blade, or Pen,
    Toil these immortal men,
Theirs is the Light supreme, which Genius wed
    To a clear spiritual Dower,
Hath ever o'er the aroused Nations shed
    Joy, faith, and power;
Whether from wrestling with the Godlike Thought,
They launch a noiseless blessing on mankind,
Or through wild streams of terrible carnage brought,
    No longer crushed and blind,
    Trampled, disheveled, gored,
They proudly lift, where kindling soul and eye
May feast upon her beauty as She stands
(Girt by the strength of her invincible Bands),
And freed through keen redemption of the sword,—
Thy worn, but radiant form, victorious Liberty!

IV.

We bow before this grandeur of the spirit;
    We worship, and adore
God's image burning through it evermore;
And thus, in awed humility to-night,*
As those who at some vast Cathedral door
Pause with hushed faces, purified desires,
    We contemplate His merit,
Who lifted Failure to the heights of Fame,
And by the side of fainting, dying Right,
Stood, as Sir Galahad pure, Sir Launcelot brave,
    The quick, indignant fires
Flushing his pale brow from the passionate mind
No strength could quell, no sophistry could bind,
Until that moment, big with mystic doom
    (Whose issue sent
    O'er the long wastes of half a continent
Electric shudders through the deepening gloom),
When in his knightly glory "Stonewall" fell,
And all our hearts sank with him; for we knew
Our staff, our bulwark broken, the fine clew
To Freedom snapped, his hands had held alone,
Through all the storms of battle overblown,—
Lost, buried, mouldering in our Hero's grave.

V.

O Soul! so simple, yet sublime!
    With faith as large, and mild
As that of some benignant, trustful child,
Who mounts to Heaven on bright, ethereal stairs
    Of tender-worded prayers,—

---

* This Ode was originally written to be delivered before a Southern patriotic association.

Yet strong as if a Titan's force were there
To rise, to act, to suffer, and to dare,—
    O Soul! that on our Time
Wrought, in the calm magnificence of power
To ends *so* noble, that an antique light
Of grace and virtue streamed along thy way,
    Until the direst hour
Of carnage caught from that immaculate ray
    A Consecration, and a Sanctity!
Thou art not dead, thou nevermore canst die,
    But wide and far,
Where'er on Christian realms the Morning Star
Flames round the spires that tower towards the sky,—
    Thy name, a household word,
In cottage homes, by palace walls, is heard,
Breathed with low murmurs, reverentially!

VI.

Even as I raise this faltering song to One,
Who now beyond the empires of the Sun,
Looks down perchance upon our mournful sphere,
With the deep pity of seraphic eyes,
Fancy unveils the Future, and I see
Millions on millions, as year follows year
Gather around our warrior's place of rest
In the green shadows of Virginian hills;
Not with the glow of martial blazonry,
    With trump and muffled drum,
    Those pilgrim millions come,
But with bowed heads, and measured footsteps slow,
As those who near the presence of a shrine,
    And feel an air divine,

All round about them blandly, sweetly blow,
While like dream-music the faint fall of rills,
    Lapsing from steep to steep,
The wood-dove 'plaining in her covert deep,
And the long whisperings of the ghostly Pine
(Like ocean-breathings borne from tides of sleep),
With every varied melody expressed
In Nature's score of solemn harmonies,
Blends with a feeling in the reverent breast,
Which cannot find a voice in mortal speech,
So deep, so deep it lies beyond the reach
Of stammering words,—the Pilgrims only know
That slumbering, O! so calmly there, below
The dewy grass, the melancholy trees,
    Moulders the dust of HIM,
By whose crystalline fame, earth's scarlet pomps grow dim,
    The crownèd Heir
    Of two majestic immortalities,
That which is earthly, and yet scarce of earth,
    Whose fruitful seeds
Were his own grand, self-sacrificing deeds,
    And that whose awful birth
Flowered into instant perfectness sublime,
    When done with toil and time,
He shook from off the raiments of his soul,
The weary conflict's desecrating dust,
For stern *reveillés*, heard the angels sing,
For battle turmoils found eternal Calm,
Laid down his sinless sword to clasp the Palm,
And where vast heavenly organ-notes outroll
Melodious thunders, 'mid the rush of wing,

And flash of plume celestial, paused in peace,
A rapture of ineffable release
To know the long fruition of the Just!

THE LITTLE WHITE GLOVE.

(FOUNDED ON AN INCIDENT OF THE LATE WAR.)

I.

THE early springtime faintly flushed the earth,
And in the woods, and by their favorite stream,
The fair wild roses blossomed modestly
Above the wave that wooed them,—there, at eve,
Philip had brought the woman that he loved,
And told his love, and bared his burning heart;
She, Constance, the shy sunbeams trembling oft
Through dewy leaves upon her golden hair,
Made him no answer,—tapped her pretty foot,
And seemed to muse. "To-morrow I depart,"
Said Philip, sadly, "for wild fields of war,—
Shall I go girt by love's invincible mail,
Stronger than mortal armor, or all stripped
Of love and hope, march reckless unto death?"
   A soft mist filled her eyes, and overflowed
In sudden rain of passion, as she stretched
Her delicate hand to his, and plighted troth
With lips more rosy than the sun-bathed flowers.
And Philip pressed the dear hand fervently,
Wherefrom in happy mood he quickly drew
A small white glove, and ere she guessed his will,

Clipped lightly from her head one golden curl,
And bound the glove, and placed it next his heart.
"Now am I safe," cried Philip, "this pure charm
Is proof against all hazard or mischance.
Here, yea, unto this self-same spot I vow
To bring it stainless back; and you shall wear
This little glove upon our marriage eve."
And Constance heard him, smiling through her tears.

II.

Another springtime faintly flushed the earth,
And in the woods, and by their favorite stream,
The fair wild roses blossomed modestly
Above the waves that wooed them; there, at eve,
Came a pale woman with wide-wandering eyes,
And tangled golden ringlets, and weak steps,
Reeling towards the streamlet's glittering marge,
She seemed phantasmal, shadowy, like the forms
By moonlight conjured from a place of graves;
There, crouching o'er the stream, she laved and laved
Some object in it with a strained regard,
And muttered fragments of distempered words,
Whereof were these: "He vowed to bring it back,
The love-charm that I gave him—my white glove—
Stainless and whole. He has not kept his oath!
O Philip! Philip! have you cast me off,
Off, like this worthless thing you send me home,
Tattered, and mildewed? Look you, what a rent,
Right through the palm!—it cannot be my glove,—
And look again! what horrid stain is here?
My glove! You placed it next your heart and swore
To keep it safe, and on this self-same spot

Return it to me on our marriage eve;
And now—and now—I *know* 'tis not my glove,
Yet Philip, sweet, it was a cruel jest,—
You surely did not mean to fright me thus?
For hark you, as I laved the loathsome thing,
To see what stain defiled it—(do not smile,
I feel that I am foolish, foolish, Philip),
But, God of heaven! I dreamed that stain was—blood!"

A FEUDAL PICTURE.

(SCENE—*The Corridor of a Palace.* PERSONS—*A young Knight and his Mentor.* TIME—*The Fourteenth Century.*)

MENTOR.

"WITH what a grace she passed us by just now!
Her delicate chin half raised, her cordial brow
A cloudless heaven of bland benignities!
What tempered lustre too in her dove's eyes,
Just touched to archness by the eyebrow's curve,
And those quick dimples which the mouth's reserve
Stir and break up, as sunlit ripples break
The cool, clear calmness of a mountain lake!
A woman in whom majesty and sweetness
Blend to such issues of serene completeness,
That to gaze on her were a prince's boon!
The calm of evening, the large pomp of noon,
Are hers; soft May morns melting into June,
Hold not such tender languishments as those

Which steep her in that dew-light of repose,
That floats a dreamy balm around the full-blown rose:—
And yet, 'tis not her beauty though so bright
(Clear moon-fire mixed with sun-flame), nor the light,
Transparent charm we feel so exquisite,
Whereby she's compassed as a wizard star
By its own life-air! 'tis not one, nor all
Of these, whereby we're mastered, Sir, and fall
Slavelike before her: doubtless such things *are*
Potent as spells,—still there's a something fine,
Subtler than hoar-rime in the faint moonshine,
More potent yet!—an undefinèd art,
'Twere vain to question: your whole being, heart,
Brain, blood, seem lapsing from you, fired and fused
In hers,—a terrible power, and if abused——
But by St. Peter! 'tis not safe to talk
Of yon weird woman! turn now! watch her walk
'Twixt the tall tiger-lilies,—there's a free,
Brave grace in every step,—but still to me,
It hath—I know not what—of covertness,
Cunning, and cruel purpose! can you guess
The picture it brings up?—a lonely rock
From which a young Bedouin guards his flock,
In the swart desert:—there's a tawny band,
A curved and tangled pathway of loose sand,
Winding above him;—the tranced airs make dim
His slumberous senses!—his great brown eyes swim
In th' mist of dreams, when gliding with mute tread
Forth from the thorn-trees, o'er his nodding head,
Moves a lithe-bodied panther;—(God! how fair
The beast is, with her moony-spotted hair,
And her deft desert paces!)—one breath more!
And you'll behold the spouting of fresh gore,

Heart-blood that's human!—can aught save him now?—
Hist! the sharp crackle of a blasted bough,
Whence flies a huge hill-eagle, rustling
O'er the boy's forehead his vast breadths of wing,
And sweeping as a half-seen shade, 'twould seem,
Betwixt his startled spirit, and its dream;
He's roused! espies his danger! at a bound
Leaps into safety where the low-set ground
Is buttressed 'neath two giant crags thereby:—
(Now hark ye! 'tis no pictured phantasy,
This scene, my Anslem! but all's true and clear
Before me, though full many a weary year
Has waxed and waned since then:—
My meaning prithee? foolish youth, beware!
There's treachery lurking in the gay parterre,
As in the hoary desert's silentness,—
And dreams with danger, death perchance behind,
May lull young sleepers in the perfumed wind,
Which hardly lifts the tiniest truant tress
It toys with coyly, of a woman's hair:—
Our sternest fates have risen in forms as fair,
As,—let us say for lack of similes,
As,—hers, who bends now with such gracious ease,
O'er her rich tulip-beds!—
                Were I the bird,
Wert THOU the shepherd ANSLEM, of my tale,
(And that thou hast not hearkened, boy, unstirred
Is clear, albeit thou need'st not wax so pale),—
What would true wisdom whisper,—now 'tis done,
My warning, and thy day-dream in the sun?—
What! why, her mandate's plain:—I hear her say,
'Young Knight! to horse! leave the Queen's Court
    to-day!'"

THE WARNING.

Patience! I yet may pierce the rind
Wherewith are shrewdly girded round
The subtle secrets of his mind;
A dark, unwholesome core is bound
Perchance within it! Sir, you see,
Men are not what they *seem* to be!

A candid mien, and plausible tongue!
A bearing calmly frank and fair,—
The tear ('twould seem) by pity wrung,
All these are his, but still, beware!—
A something strange, false, unbegot
Of virtue, whispers, trust him not:—

But yesterday, his mask (I know
He wears one), for a moment's space,
By chance dropped off, and swift below
The smile just waning on his face,
I caught a look, flashed sudden, keen
As lightning, which he deemed unseen:

I will not pause to tell thee what
That look betrayed! enough I think,
To smite the spirit cold and hot,
By turns,—and make one inly shrink
From contact with a soul that keeps
Such wild-fire smouldering in its deeps:

So friend, be warned! he is not one
Thy youth should trust, for all his smiles,
Frank foreheads, genial as the Sun,
May hide a thousand treacherous wiles,
And tones, like music's honeyed flow,
May work (God knows!) the bitterest woe!

DRIFTING.

I HAVE settled at last in a sombre nook,
In the far-off heart of the Norland hills,
There's a dark pine forest before my gates,
And behind is the voice of rills
That murmur all day, and murmur all night,
Through the tangled copses green and lone,
Where, couched in the depths of the shadowy leaves,
The wood-dove makes her moan.

My home is a castle ancient and worn,
With hoary walls, and with crumbling floors,
And the Burglar-Winds their entrance force
Through the cobwebbed panes and doors.
I can hardly say that a roof is mine,
For whene'er the mountain tempests rise,
A deluge is poured through its countless rents,
Wide open to air and skies!

Ah! Nature alone keeps a wholesome mien,
In the midst of a squalor wildly bare,

And I draw sometimes from her bounteous breast
Brief balms for the heart's despair;
All *human* friends that were loyal have died,
And the false and treacherous only stay,
To poison the soul with their serpent tongues
In my fortune's dull decay!

Distant and dim in the perishing past
Grow the joys that made its springtime sweet,
And the last of the saving angels—Hope—
Hath spurned my lot with her shining feet;
Ambition is dead, and if Love survives,
Her lip, it is pale, and her eyes forlorn
As beams of the waning stars that melt
In a clouded winter's morn.

I have met my fate as a man should meet
What cannot be vanquished, nor put aside,
I have striven with spirit and force to stem
Its rushing and mighty tide;
But the Godlike nerve, and the iron will,
They were not granted to me, I say,
And therefore a waif on an angry sea,
I am drifting, drifting away!

Ay! drifting, and drifting, and drifting away,
Not a hand upraised, nor a cry for aid;
And hoarser the voice of the storm-wind swells,
And darker the wild night-shade;
There are breakers ahead that will crush me soon,
How much, O God! do thy creatures bear!
I marvel if somewhere, in Heaven or Hell,
This riddle of life grows clear!

SONNET.

CAROLINA.

THAT fair young land which gave me birth is dead !
Lost as a fallen star that quivering dies
Down the pale pathway of Autumnal skies,
A vague faint radiance flickering where it fled ;
All she hath wrought, all she hath planned or said,
Her golden eloquence, her high emprise,
Wrecked, on the languid shore of Lethe lies,
While cold Oblivion veils her piteous head :*
O mother ! loved and loveliest ! debonair
As some brave Queen of antique chivalries,—

---

* This may be esteemed an *exaggeration;* but really it is the sober and melancholy truth. The fame of the great Statesmen and Orators, for example, who once flourished in South Carolina, and made her name illustrious from one end of the Union to the other, is fast becoming a mere shadowy tradition. With a single exception, their works have never been collected for publication, nor have their lives been written, unless in the most fragmentary and imperfect fashion. The period during which these things might have been rightly done has forever passed.

Thus, over their genius and performances, as over their native State, —the Carolina of old,—oblivion, day by day, is more darkly gathering. If elements of a new political birth exist in that unfortunate section, they are *now* hopelessly confused and chaotic!

While the Past recedes, becoming momently more ghostly and phantasmal, the Future is wrapped in thick clouds and darkness! Where, indeed, is the prophet or son of a prophet who can predict the nature of that new Polity destined to rise from the old institutions and the defunct civilization?

Thy beauty's blasted like thy desolate coasts;—
Where now thy lustrous form, thy shining hair?
Where thy bright presence, thine imperial eyes?
Lost in dim shadows of the realm of Ghosts!

SONNET.

LEIGH HUNT.

"Leigh Hunt *loves everything:* he catches the sunny side of everything, and—except a few polemical antipathies—finds everything beautiful."—HENRY CRABB ROBINSON.

DESPITE misfortune, poverty, the dearth
Of simplest justice to his heart and brain,—
This gracious Optimist lived not in vain;
Rather, he made a partial Heaven of Earth;
For whatsoe'er of pure and cordial birth
In body or soul, dawned on him, he was fain
To bless and love, as an immortal gain,
A thing divine, of fair immaculate worth:—
The clearest, cleanest nature given to man
In these, our latter days, methinks was his,
With instincts which alone did bring him bliss;
All life he viewed as one long, luminous plan
Wherein God's love and wisdom meet and kiss,—
His sole brave creed, the creed Samaritan!

SONNET.

In yonder grim, funereal forest lies
A foul lagoon, o'erfilmed by dust and slime,
Hidden and ghastly, like a thought of crime
In some stern soul, kept secret from men's eyes;
But if, perchance, a healthful breeze should rise,
And part those stifling boughs, sweet morning's prime,
And the fair flush of evening's cordial clime,
Reflect therein the calmly glorious skies:
Is't so with man? holds not the darkened breast,
Turbid, corrupt, o'ergrown by worldliness,
One little spot whereon love's smile may rest?
Lo! a pure impulse breathes, the sin-clouds part,
The grief-defilements melt in hopes that bless,
And pour God's quickening sunshine on the heart!

SONNET.

SOUL ADVANCES.

He, who with fervent toil and will austere,
His innate forces, and high faculties,
Develops ever, with firm aim, and wise,—
He *only* keeps his spiritual vision clear;
To him earth's treacherous shadows shift and veer
Like idle mists o'ercrowding windless skies,

Where through ofttimes to purged and prayerful eyes,
The steadfast heavens seem beckoning calm and
        near:—
Still, o'er life's rugged heights, with many a slip,
And painful pause he journeys, and sad fall,
Toward death's dark strand, washed by a mystic sea;—
There her worn cable straining to be free,
He sees, and enters Faith's majestic ship,
To sail—*where'er the voice of God may call!*

ODE TO SLEEP.

BEYOND the sunset, and the amber sea
To the lone depths of Ether, cold and bare,
Thy influence, Soul of all tranquillity,
Hallows the Earth, and awes the reverent air;
Yon laughing rivulet quells its silvery tune,—
The Pines, like priestly watchers tall and grim,
Stand mute, against the pensive twilight dim,
Breathless to hail the advent of the Moon;
From the white beach the Ocean falls away
Coyly, and with a thrill; the sea-birds dart
Ghostlike from out the distance, and depart
With a gray fleetness, moaning the dead Day;
The wings of Silence overfolding space,
Droop with dusk grandeur from the heavenly steep,
And through the stillness gleams thy starry face,
        Serenest Angel—Sleep!

ODE TO SLEEP.

Come! woo me here, amid these flowery charms,
Breathe on my eyelids; press thy odorous lips
Close to mine own, enwreathe me in thine arms,
And cloud my spirit with thy sweet eclipse;—
No dreams! no dreams! keep back the motley throng,—
For such are girded round with ghastly might,
And sing low burdens of despondent song,
Decked in the mockery of a lost delight;—
I ask Oblivion's balsam! the mute peace
Toned to still breathings, and the gentlest sighs,—
Not music woven of rarest harmonies
Could yield me such elysium of release:—
The tones of Earth are weariness,—not only
'Mid the loud mart, and in the walks of trade,
But where the mountain Genius broodeth lonely,
In the cool pulsing of the sylvan shade:—
Then, bear me far into thy noiseless land,
Surround me with thy silence, deep on deep,
      Until serene I stand
Close by a duskier country, and more grand,
Mysterious Solitude, than thine, O Sleep!

As he whose veins a feverous frenzy burns,
Whose life-blood withers in the fiery drouth,—
Feebly, and with a languid longing, turns
To the spring breezes gathering from the South,—
So, feebly, and with languid longing, I
Turn to thy wished Nepenthe, and implore
The golden dimness, the purpureal gloom
Which haunt thy poppied realm, and make the shore
Of thy dominion balmy with all bloom:—
In the clear gulfs of thy serene Profound,

Worn Passions sink to quiet, Sorrows pause,
Suddenly fainting to still-breathèd rest;—
Thou own'st a magical atmosphere, which awes
The memories seething in the turbulent breast;
Which muffling up the sharpness of all sound
Of mortal lamentation,—solely bears
The silvery minor toning of our woe,
All mellowed to harmonious underflow,—
Soft as the sad farewells of dying years,—
Lulling as sunset showers that veil the West,
    And sweet as Love's last tears
When overwelling hearts do mutely weep:—
O Griefs! O wailings! your tempestuous madness,
Merged in a regal quietude of sadness,
Wins a strange glory by the streams of Sleep!

Then woo me here amid these flowery charms,
Breathe on my eyelids, press thy odorous lips
Close to mine own,—enfold me in thine arms,
And cloud my spirit with thy sweet eclipse;—
And while from waning depth to depth I fall,
Down lapsing to the utmost depths of all,—
Till wan forgetfulness obscurely stealing,
Creeps like an incantation on the soul,—
And o'er the slow ebb of my conscious life
Dies the thin flush of the last conscious feeling,—
And like abortive thunder, the dull roll
Of sullen passions ebbs far, far away,—
O Angel! loose the chords which cling to strife,
Sever the gossamer bondage of my breath,—
And let me pass gently as winds in May,
From the dim realm which owns thy shadowy sway,
To THY diviner Sleep, O sacred Death!

SONG.

O! to be
By the sea, the sea!
While a brave Nor'wester's blowing,
With a swirl on the lea,
Of cloud-foam free,
And a spring-tide deeply flowing!
With the low moon red and large,
O'er the flushed horizon's marge,
And a little pink hand in mine,
On the sands in the long moonshine!

O! to be
By the sea, the sea!
With the wind full west and dying,
With a single star
O'er the misty bar,
And the dim waves dreamily sighing!
O! to be there, but there!
With my sweet Love nestling near!
Near, near, till her heart-throbs blend with mine,
Through the balmy hush of the night's decline,
On the glimmering beach, in the soft star-shine!

HOPES AND MEMORIES.

Our hopes in youth are like those roseate shadows
Cast by the sunlight on the dewy grass
When first the fair Morn opes her sapphire eyes;
They seem gigantic and yet graceful shades,
Touched with bright color. As our sun of life
Rises towards meridian, less and less
Grow the bright tremulous shadows, till at last,
In the hot dust and noontide of our day,
They glimmer to blank nothingness. Again,
That grand climacteric passed, the shadows gleam
Bright still, perchance (if our past deeds be pure),—
Bright still, but all reversed! Eastward they point,
Lengthening and lengthening ever toward the dawn;
For hopes have then grown memories, whose strange life
Deepens and deepens as the sunset dies.

WIDDERIN'S RACE.

(AUSTRALIAN.)

(The incidents of the following sketch will be found in "The Recollections of Geoffrey Hamlin," by Henry Kingsley.)

"A horse amongst ten thousand! on the verge,
The extremest verge of equine life he stands;
Yet mark his action, as those wild young colts
Freed from the stock-yard gallop whinnying up;

See how he trots towards them,—nose in air,
Tail arched, and his still sinewy legs out-thrown
In gallant grace before him! A brave beast
As ever spurned the moorland, ay, and more,—
He bore me once,—such words but smite the truth
I' the outer ring, while vivid memory wakes,
Recalling now, the passion and the pain,—
He bore me once from earthly Hell to Heaven!

"The sight of fine old Widderin (that's his name,
Caught from a peak, the topmost rugged peak
Of tall Mount Widderin, towering to the North
Most like a steed's head, with full nostrils blown,
And ears pricked up),—the sight of Widderin brings
That day of days before me, whose strange hours
Of fear and anguish, ere the sunset, changed
To hours of such content, and full-veined joy,
As Heaven can give our mortal lives but once.

"Well, here's the story: While yon bush-fires sweep
The distant ranges, and the river's voice
Pipes a thin treble through the heart of Drouth,—
While the red Heaven like some huge caldron's top
Seems with the heat a-simmering, better far
In place of riding tilt 'gainst such a sun,
Here in the safe veranda's flowery gloom,
To play the dwarfish Homer to a song,
Whereof myself am hero:

                    "Two decades
Have passed since that wild autumn-time when last
The convict hordes from near Van Diemen freed
By force or fraud, swept, like a blood-red fire,

Inland from beach to mountain, bent on raid
And rapine; fiends o' th' lowest pit, they spared
Nor sex, nor age, nor infancy; the vulture
Followed their track, and a black smoke like hell's
Hung its foul reek above each home accursed,
Sacked by their greed, or ravished by their lust.
Their crimes were monstrous, weird, unutterable,
Not to be hinted, save in awe-struck whispers
Dropped by dark hearthstones, far from maidens' ears,
In the blank, silent midnight! all the land
Uprose to seek, confront, and decimate
These devils spawned of Tophet; but their bands
At the first bruit of battle, the first clang
Of sabres girding honest loins, and champ
Of horse-bits held by manly hands that burned
To smite them, hip and thigh,—fled, disappeared,
And crouched in hiding, wheresoe'er the Earth,
By wave and hillside, forest, and bleak tarn,
Vouchsafed to shield them; as the time rolled on,
Our fears grew lighter, and all dread was quelled,
When on a morning, 'mid the outmost reefs
Of rough Cape Bolling, our chief herdsman found
The carcass of a huge boat overturned,
All stoven, and firmly wedged between the jaws
Of monster rocks, whereby three bodies lay,
Splashing and gurgling in the refluent tides,
Well known as corses of three desperate men,
The outlaws' leaders; thereupon 'twas deemed,—
And all must own with fairest likelihood,—
That glutted by their vengeance, or spurred on
By hopes of rapine, beckoning otherwhere,—
The whole foul crew embarking, had been seized
By wind and wave, God's Executioners,

The pitiless Doomsmen of the wrath of Heaven,—
And so, crushed out of being, and made less
Than the vile seaweed dabbling in the surf.

"Thenceforth, our caution cooled; save here and there,
At critical mountain-passes, or lone caves,
And sheltered inlets of the wild Southwest,
No sentinels watched; and wherefore should they watch?
The storm had threatened, broken, and was passed!

"So, in late Autumn,—'twas a marvelous morn,
With breezes from the calm snow-river borne
That touched the air, and stirred it into thrills,
Mysterious and mesmeric, a bright mist
Lapping the landscape like a golden trance,
Swathing the hilltops with fantastic veils,
And o'er the moorland-ocean quivering light
As gossamer threads drawn down the forest aisles
At dewy dawning,—on this marvelous morn,
I, with four comrades, in this self-same spot,
Watched the fair scene, and drank the spicy airs,
That held a subtler spirit than our wine,
And talked and laughed, and mused in idleness,—
Weaving vague fancies, as our pipe-wreaths curled
Fantastic in the sunlight! I, with head
Thrown back, and cushioned snugly, and with eyes
Intent on one grotesque and curious cloud,
Puffed upward, that now seemed to take the shape
Of a Dutch tulip, now a Turk's face topped
By folds on folds of turban limitless,—
Heard suddenly, just as the clock chimed one,
To melt in musical echoes up the hills,
Quick footsteps on the graveled path without,—

Steps of the couriers of calamity,—
So my heart told me,—ere with blanched regards,
Two stalwart herdsmen on our threshold paused,
Panting, with lips that writhed, and awful eyes;—
A breath's space in each other's eyes we glared,
Then, swift as interchange of lightning thrusts
In deadly combat, question and reply
Clashed sharply, 'What! the Rangers?' 'Ay, by Heaven!
And loosed in force,—the hell-hounds!' 'Whither bound?'
I stammered, hoarsely. 'Bound,' the elder said,
'Southward!—four stations had they sacked and burnt,
And now, drunk, furious——' but I stopped to hear
No more; with booming thunder in mine ears,
And blood-flushed eyes, I rushed to Widderin's side,
Drew tight the girths, upgathered curb and rein,
And sprang to horse ere yet our laggard friends,—
Now trooping from the green veranda's shade,—
Could dream of action!

"Love had winged my will,
For to the southward, fair Garoopna held
My all of hope, life, passion; she whose hair
(Its tiniest strand of waving, witch-like gold)
Had caught my heart, entwined, and bound it fast,
As 'twere some sweet enchantment's heavenly net!

"I only gave a hand-wave in farewell,
Shot by, and o'er the endless moorland swept
(Endless it seemed, as those weird, measureless plains,
Which, in some nightmare vision, stretch and stretch
Towards infinity!) like some lone ship

O'er wastes of sailless waters: now, a Pine,
The beacon Pine gigantic, whose grim crown
Signals the far land-mariner from out
Gaunt boulders of the gray-backed Organ hill,
Rose on my sight, a mistlike, wavering orb,—
The while, still onward, onward, onward still,
With motion winged, elastic, equable,
Brave Widderin cleaved the air-tides, tossed aside
The winds as waves, their swift, invisible breasts,
Hissing with foamlike noise when pressed and pierced
By that keen head and fiery-crested form!

"The lonely shepherd guardian on the plains,
Watching his sheep through languid, half-shut eyes,
Looked up, and marveled, as we passed him by,
Thinking, perchance, it was a glorious thing,
So dressed, so booted, so caparisoned,
To ride such bright blood-coursers unto death!
Two sun-blacked Natives, slumbering in the grass,
Just rose betimes to 'scape the trampling hoofs,
And hurled hot curses at me as I sped;
While here and there, the timid kangaroo
Blundered athwart the mole-hills, and in puffs
Of steamy dust-cloud vanished like a mote!

"Onward, still onward, onward, onward still!
And lo! thank Heaven, the mighty Organ hill,
That seemed a dim blue cloudlet at the start,
Hangs in aërial, fluted cliffs aloft,—
And still as through the long, low glacis borne,
Beneath the gorge borne ever at wild speed,
I saw the mateless mountain eagle wheel
Beyond the stark height's topmost pinnacle;

I heard his shriek of rage and rivin die
Deep down the desolate dells, as far behind
I left the gorge, and far before me swept
Another plain, tree-bordered now, and bound
By the clear river gurgling o'er its bed.

"By this, my panting, but unconquered steed
Had thrown his small head backward, and his breath
Through the red nostrils burst in labored sighs;
I bent above his outstretched neck, I threw
My quivering arms about him, murmuring low,
'Good horse! brave heart! a little longer bear
The strain, the travail; and thenceforth for thee
Free pastures all thy days, till death shall come!
Ah, many and many a time, my noble Bay,
Her lily hand hath wandered through thy mane,
Patted thy rainbow neck, and brought thee ears
Of daintiest corn from out the farm-house loft,—
Help, help to save her now!'

"I'll vow the brute
Heard me, and comprehended what he heard!
He shook his proud crest madly, and his eye
Turned for a moment sideways, flashed in mine
A lightning gleam, whose fiery language said,
'I know my lineage, will not shame my sire,—
My sire, who rushed triumphant 'twixt the flags,
And frenzied thousands, when on Epsom downs
Arcturus won the Derby!—no, nor shame
My granddam, whose clean body, half enwrought
Of air, half fire, through swirls of desert sand
Bore Shiëk Abdallah headlong on his prey!'

"At last came forest shadows, and the road
Winding through bush and bracken, and at last
The hoarse stream rumbling o'er its quartz-sown crags.

"No, no! stanch Widderin! pause not now to drink;
An hour hence, and thy dainty nose shall dip
In richest wine, poured jubilantly forth
To quench thy thirst, my Beauty! but press on,
Nor heed these sparkling waters. God! my brain's
On fire once more! an instant tells me all;
All!—life or death,—salvation or despair!—
For yonder, o'er the wild grass-matted slope
The house stands, or it stood but yesterday.

"A Titan cry of inarticulate joy
I raised, as calm and peaceful in the sun,
Shone the fair cottage, and the garden-close,
Wherein, white-robed, unconscious, sat my Love
Lilting a low song to the birds and flowers.
She heard the hoof-strokes, saw me, started up,
And with her blue eyes wider than their wont,
And rosy lips half tremulous, rushed to meet
And greet me swiftly. 'Up, dear Love!' I cried,
'The Convicts, the Bush-Rangers!—let us fly!'
Ah, then and there you should have seen her, friend,
My noble, beauteous Helen! not a tear,
Nor sob, and scarce a transient pulse-quiver,
As, clasping hand in hand, her fairy foot
Lit like a small bird on my horseman's boot,
And up into the saddle, lithe and light,
Vaulting she perched, her bright curls round my face!

"We crossed the river, and, dismounting, led

O'er the steep slope of blended rock and turf,
The wearied horse, and there behind a Tor
Of castellated bluestone, paused to sweep
With young keen eyes the broad plain stretched afar,
Serene and Autumn-tinted at our feet:
'Either,' said I, 'these devils have gone East,
To meet with bloodhound Desborough in his rage
Between the granite passes of Luxorme,
Or else,—dear Christ! my Helen, low! stoop low!'
(These words were hissed in horror, for just then,
'Twixt the deep hollows of the river-vale,
The miscreants, with mixed shouts and curses, poured
Down through the flinty gorge tumultuously,
Seeming, we thought, in one fierce throng to charge
Our hiding-place.) I seized my Widderin's head,
Blindfolding him, for with a single neigh
Our fate were sealed o' th' instant! As they rode,
Those wild, foul-languaged demons by our lair,
Scarce twelve yards off, my troubled steed shook wide
His streaming mane, stamped on the earth, and pawed
So loudly, that the sweat of agony rolled
Down my cold forehead; at which point, I felt
My arm clutched, and a voice I did not know,
Dropped the low murmur from pale, shuddering lips,
'O God! if in those brutal hands I fall,
Living, look not into your mother's face
Or *any* woman's more!'

"What time had passed
Above our bowed heads, we pent, pinioned there
By awe and nameless horror, who shall tell?
Minutes, perchance, by mortal measurement,
Eternity by heart-throbs!—when at length

We turned, and eyes of mutual wonder raised,
We gazed on alien faces, haggard, worn,
And strange of feature as the faces born
In fever and delirium! Were we saved?
We scarce could comprehend it, till, from out
The neighboring oak-wood, rode our friends at speed,
With clang of steel and eyebrows bent in wrath.
But warned betimes, the wily ruffians fled
Far up the forest-coverts, and beyond
The dazzling snow-line of the distant hills,
Their yells of fiendish laughter pealing faint,
And fainter from the cloudland, and the mist
That closed about them like an ash-gray shroud:
Yet were these wretches marked for imminent death:
The next keen sunrise pierced the savage gorge,
To which we tracked them, where, mere beasts at bay,—
Grimly they fought, and brute by brute they fell."

OCTOBER.

AFAR from the city, its cark and care,—
Thank God! I am cosily seated here,
    On this night of hale October,—
While the flames leap high on the roaring hearth,
And voices, the dearest to me on earth,
Ring out in the music of household mirth,
    For the time is blithe October!

There's something,—but *what* I can scarce divine,—
Perchance 'tis the breath like a potent wine,—
    Of the cordial, clear October,—

Which makes, when the jovial month comes round,
The life-blood bloom, and the pulses bound,
And the soul spring forth like a monarch crown'd,—
    God's grace on the brave October!

Come, Sweetheart! open your choicest bin,
For who, I would marvel, could deem it sin,
    On this night of keen October,
To quaff one health to his ruddy cheer,
On the golden edge of the waning year,
To his eyes so bright, and his cheeks so clear,—
    Our bluff "King Hal,"—October?

Away with Rhenish and light Champagne!
'Tis not in these we must pledge the reign
    Of the stout old Lord,—October;
But in mighty stoups of the "mountain dew,"
With "beads" like tears in an eye of blue,
But tears of a laughter, sound and true,
    As thine honest heart, October!

He brought me love and he brought me health,
He brought me *all* but the curse of wealth,
    This kindly and free October;
And forever and aye I will bless his name,
While his winds blow fresh, and his sunsets flame,
And the whole earth burns with his crimson fame,
    This Prince of the months,—October!

HERE AND THERE.*

HERE the warm sunshine fills
Like wine of gods the deepening, cup-shaped dells,
Embossed with marvelous flowers; the happy rills
Roam through the autumnal fields whose rich increase
Of gathered grain smiles under heavens of peace;
    While many a bird-song swells
From glades of neighboring woodlands, cool and fair,—
    Content and Peace are *here*.

THERE the wild Battle's wrath
Thunders from castled height to storied plain,
Plows with red lightning-bolts its terrible path,
And sows the abhorrent seeds of blood and death,
Blown far on Desolation's tameless breath,—
    While for autumnal grain
Time reaps the harvest of a bleak despair,—
    God's curse consumes them *there*.

HERE jovial children play
Beneath the latest vine-leaves; innocent kings,
And blissful queens,—on them the matron Day,
Like a sweet mother, drops her kisses light;
The very clouds some secret joy makes bright,—
    And round us clings and clings
With Ariel arms, the season's influence rare,—
    Heaven's heart beats near us *here*.

---

* Written during the war between France and Germany.

There Love bemoans its lost,
Countless as seaside sands; all joys of life
Rest locked and stirless in the blood-red frost;
Ye drums roll out, shrill clarions peal your parts!
Ye cannot drown the wail of broken hearts,
  Nor still that spiritual strife
Which thrills through Victory's voice its death-notes drear,—
  Dear Christ, soothe, save them *there!*

ODE

IN HONOR OF THE BRAVERY AND SACRIFICES OF THE SOLDIERS OF THE SOUTH.

With bayonets slanted in the glittering light,
  With solemn roll of drums,
With star-lit banners rustling wings of might,
  The knightly concourse comes!
The flower and fruit of all the tropic lands,
The unsheathed brightness of their stainless brands
  Blazing in courtly hands,—
One glorious soul within those thousand eyes,—
One aim, one hope, one impulse from the skies,—
  While silent, awed and dumb,
A nation waits the end in dread surmise,
  They come! they come!

The summer flaunts her vivid leaves above
  The unwonted scene,—

THE SOLDIERS OF THE SOUTH.

The summer heavens embrace with smiles of love
    The hill-slopes green;
Far in the uppermost realms of silent air
Peace sits enthroned and happy, but on earth
The cymbals clash, and the shrill trumpets blare,
And Death, like some grim Mower on the plain,
    Topped by the ripened grain,
Whets his keen scythe, and shakes it fearfully!

Our serried lines march sternly to the front,
Where decked as if they rose to celebrate
    A joyous festal morn,
In glistening pomp and splendid blazonry,
    Slow moving as in scorn
Of those weak bands that guard the pass below,
Come gorgeous, flushed and proud, the cohorts of the
    foe!

They wheel! deploy, are stationed, down the cleft
    Of the long gorge their signal thunders run!
A sullen answer echoes from our left
    And the great fight's begun!
O! who shall picture the immortal fray?
Our Southern host that day
Breasted the onset of the invading sea
With wills of adamant; but stern-weighted strength,
Like waves by some infernal alchemy
Hardened, transformed to solid metal, burning
At white heat as they struck, and aye returning
Hotter and more resistless than before
(All flecked atop with foam of human gore),
Pierced here and there our crumbling ranks at length,
    Which as a mountain shore,

Rock-ribbed and iron founded, still had stood,
    And outward hurled
In bloody sprayings, that tremendous flood
Which, with wild charge and furious brunt on brunt,
Had dashed against us like a fiery world!

Unceasing still poured on the fateful tide,
And plumèd victory ever seemed to ride
On the red billows of the northland war!
    Our glory and pride
Had fallen,—fallen in the terrible van,—
Like wine the life-streams ran;
"Back! back!" cried one (it was the voice of Bee,
Lifted in wrath and bitter agony),
"We're driven backward!" unto whom there came
An answer, like the rush of steady flame,
'Twixt ribs of iron, "We will give them yet
    The bayonet!
The sharp edge of the Southern bayonet!"
At which the other's face flushed up, and caught
Light like a warrior-angel's, and he sprang
To the front rank, while swift as passionate thought
Leaped forth his sword, and this high summons rang:
    "See! see! where fixed and grand,
Like a stone wall the braves of Jackson stand!"
"Forward!" and on he rushed with quivering breath,
    On to his Spartan death!

Unceasing still poured down the fateful tide,
And plumèd victory ever seemed to ride
O'er the red billows of the northland war!
    When faint and far,

Far on our left there rose a sound that thrilled
All souls, and even the battle's thunderous pulse
(Or so we deemed), for briefest space was stilled;
A sound, low hissing as a meteor-tar,
But gathering depth of volume, till it burst
    In one great flamelike cheer,
That seemed to rend and lift the cloud accurst,
    The poisonous-clinging cloud
    That wrapped us in its shroud,
While wounded men leaped on their feet to hear,
And dying men upraised their eyes to see
How on the conflict's lowering canopy,
Dawned the first rainbow hues of victory!

    Have you watched the Condor leap
    From his proud Andean rock,
    And with hurtling pinions sweep
    On the valley-pasturing flock?
    Have you watched an Eygre vast
    On the rude September blast
    Roll adown with curved crest
    O'er the low sands of the West?
    O! thus and thus they came
    (Four thousand men and more),
    Hearts, faces,—all aflame,
    And the grandeur of their wrath
    Whirled the Tyrant from their path
    As the frightened rack is driven
    By the unleashed winds in heaven;
    Then, maddened, tossed about
    In a reckless, hopeless rout,
    The Northern army fled
    O'er their dying and their dead,

And the Southern steel flashed out,
And their vengeful points were red
With the hot heart's tide that flowed
Where they sabred as they rode!
And the news sped on apace
(Where the Rulers, in their place,
Sat jubilant, one and all),
Till a shadow seemed to fall
Round their joyance like a pall,
And the inmost Senate-hall
Pealed an echo of disgrace!
At the set of July's sun
They stood quivering and undone,
For the eagle standards waned and the Southern "stars"
    had won!

Thus loomed serene and large
Upon that desperate contest's lurid marge
Our orb of destiny; millions of hearts
Throb with bold exultation,
Till there starts
From mountain fastness, and from waving plain,
From wooded swamp and mist-encircled main,
From hamlet, city, field,
And the rich midland weald,
The spirit of the antique Hero Time!
O! 'twas a sight sublime
To watch the upheaval of the popular soul,—
The stormy gathering,—the majestic roll
Upward of its wild forces, by the awe
Of Right and Justice steadied into law!
Faith lent our cause its heavenly consecration!
    Hope its omnipotent might!
And Fame stood ready, with her flowers of light,

To crown alike the living and the dead,
While in the broadening firmament o'erhead
We seemed to read the fiat of our fate,
   "Ye are baptized,—a Nation!
Amongst the freest, free,—amongst the mightiest, great!"
An ominous hush! and then the scattered clouds
    In the dark northern heaven
(Clouds of a deadlier strife),
    Urged by the poison wind
    Of rage and rapine, sullenly combined,
Charged with the bolts of ruin! what were shrouds,
Crimsoned with gore? the widowed spirit riven?
The desecration of God's gift of life,
To that one thought (three fiery strands uniting,
    Hot from a Hadèan loom),
"Conquest!" "Revenge!" "Supremacy?" The blighting
Of untold promises, the grief, the gloom,
The desolate madness and the anguish blind,
    All spreading on and on
From murdered sire to subjugated son,
Were less than nothing to the arrogant pride
Which treaties, compacts, honor, laws defied,
And aimed above the wrecks of temple and tower
To rear the symbols of its merciless power!

    Four deadly years we fought,
Ringed by a girdle of unfaltering fire,
That coiled and hissed in lessening circles nigher.
    Blood dyed the Southern wave;
From ocean border to calm inland river,
There was no pause, no peace, no respite ever.

Blood of our bravest brave
Drenched in a scarlet rain the western lea,
Swelled the hoarse waters of the Tennessee,
Incarnadined the gulfs, the lakes, the rills,
And from a hundred hills
Steamed in a mist of slaughter to the skies,
Shutting all hope of heaven from mortal eyes.
The Beaufort blooms were withered on the stem;
    The fair gulf city in a single night
    Lost her imperial diadem;
And wheresoe'er men's troubled vision sought,
They viewed MIGHT towering o'er the humbled crest
    of RIGHT!

But for a time, but for a time, O God!
The innate forces of our knightly blood
Rallied, and by the mount, the fen, the flood,
    Upraised the tottering standards of our race.
O grand Virginia! though thy glittering glaive
Lies sullied, shattered in a ruthless grave,
How it flashed once! They dug their trenches deep
(The implacable foe), they ranged their lines of wrath;
But watchful ever on the imminent path,
    Thy steel-clad genius stood;
North, South, East, West,—they strove to pierce thy
    shield;
Thou would'st not yield!
Until,—unconquered, yea, unconquered still,—
NATURE'S weakened forces answered not thy WILL,
And gored with wound on wound,
Thy fainting limbs and forehead sought the ground;
And with thee the young nation fell, a pall
Solemn and rayless, covering one and all!

God's ways are marvelous; here we stand to-day
Discrowned, and shorn, in wildest disarray,
The mock of earth! yet never shone the sun
On sterner deeds, or nobler victories won.
Not in the field alone; ah, come with me
To the dim bivouac by the winter's sea;
Mark the fair sons of courtly mothers crouch
O'er flickering fires; but gallant still, and gay
As on some bright parade; or mark the couch
    In reeking hospitals, whereon is laid
The latest scion of a line perchance,
Whose veins were royal; close your blurred romance,
Blurred by the dropping of a maudlin tear,
And watch the manhood here;
    That firm but delicate countenance,
Distorted sometimes by an awful pang,
Borne in meek patience; when the trumpets rang
"To horse!" but yester-morn, that ardent boy
Sprung to his charger, thrilled with hope and joy
To the very finger-tips, and now he lies,
The shadows deepening in those falcon eyes,
    But calm and undismayed,
As if the Death that chills him, brow and breast,
Were some fond bride who whispered, "Let us rest!"

Enough! 'tis over! the last gleam of hope
Hath melted from our mournful horoscope,—
    Of all, of all bereft,
    Only to us are left
Our buried heroes and their matchless deeds;
These cannot pass; they hold the vital seeds
Which in some far, untracked, unvisioned hour
May burst to vivid bud and glorious flower.

Meanwhile, upon the nation's broken heart
Her martyrs sleep. O! dearer far to her,
Than if each son, a wreathèd conqueror,
    Rode in triumphant state
    The loftiest crest of fate;
O! dearer far, because outcast and low,
She yearns above them in her awful woe.
One spring its tender blooms
Hath lavished richly by those hallowed tombs;
One summer its imperial largess spread
Along our heroes' bed;
One autumn wailing with funereal blast,
The withered leaves and pallid dust amassed
All round about them, till bleak winter now
Hangs hoar-frost on the grasses, and the bough
    In dreary woodlands seems to thrill and start,
Thrill to the anguish of the wind that raves
Across those lonely, desolated graves!
    1866.

SONNET.

ILLEGITIMATE.

THE maiden SPRING came laughing down the dales,
Her fair brows arched, and on her rosebud mouth,
The balm and beauty of the lustrous *South;*
Through soft green fields, from hills to happy vales,
She tripped, her small feet twinkling in the sun;
Her delicate finger raised with girlish mirth,
Pointed at graybeard *Winter*, who, in dearth,

Toiled toward his couch, his long day labor done;
Ah no, not done! for hark! a sudden wind,
Death-laden, sweeps from realms of arctic sky,
And blurred with storm, the morn grows crazed and blind;
Then, WINTER mocking, backward turns apace,
Where pallid Spring, all vainly strives to fly,
And with brute buffet scars her shrinking face!

SONNET.

VERNAL PICTURES (WITHOUT AND WITHIN).

AMID fresh roses wandering, and the soft
And delicate wealth of apple-blossoms spread
In tender spirals of blent white and red,
Round the fair spaces of our blooming croft,—
This morn I caught the gurgling note, so oft
Heard in the golden spring-tides that are dead,—
The Swallow's note, murmuring of winter fled,
Dropped silverly from passionless calms aloft:—
"O heart!" I said, "thy vernal depths unclose,
That mirror Nature's; warm airs, come and go
Of whispering Ardors o'er Thought's budded rose,
And half-hid flowers of sweet philosophy;
While now upglancing, now borne swift and low,
SONG like the swallow darts through Fancy's sky."

WELCOME TO WINTER.

Now, with wild and windy roar,
Stalwart Winter comes once more,—
O'er our roof-tree thunders loud,
And from edges of black cloud
Shakes his beard of hoary gold,
Like a tangled torrent rolled
Down the sky-rifts, clear and cold!

Hark! his trumpet summons rings,
Potent as a warrior-king's;
Till the forces of our blood
Rise to lusty hardihood,
And our summer's languid dreams
Melt, like form-wreaths, down the streams,
When the fierce northeasters roll,
Raving from the frozen pole.

Nobler hopes, and keener life,
Quicken in his breath of strife;
Through the snow-storms and the sleet
On he stalks with armèd feet,
While the sounding clash of hail
Clanging on his icy mail,
Stirs whate'er of generous might
Time hath left us in his flight,
And our yearning pulses thrill
For some grand achievement still!

Lord of ice-bound sea and land,
Let me grasp thy kingly hand,—

And from thy great heart and bold,
Hecla-warm, though all is cold
Round about thee, catch the fire
Of my lost youth's brave desire;
Let me,—in the war with wrong,—
Like thy storms, be swift and strong,—
Gloomy griefs, and coward cares,
Broods of 'wildering, dark despairs,
Making all life's glory dim,—
Let me rend them, limb from limb,
As the forest-boughs are rent
When thou wak'st the firmament,
And with savage shriek and groan
All the wildwood's overthrown!

WILL.

Your face, my boy, when six months old,
   We propped you laughing in a chair,—
And the sun-artist caught the gold
   Which rippled o'er your waving hair!
And deftly shadowed forth the while
That blooming cheek, that roguish smile,
     Those dimples seldom still:
The tiny, wondering, wide-eyed elf!
Now, *can* you recognize yourself
     In that small portrait, Will?

I glance at it, then turn to you,
   Where in your healthful ease you stand,
No Beauty,—but a youth as true,
   And pure as any in the land!

For Nature, through fair sylvan ways,
Hath led and gladdened all your days,
    Kept free from sordid ill;
Hath filled your veins with blissful fire,
And winged your instincts to aspire
    Sunward, and Godward, Will!

Long-limbed and lusty, with a stride
    That leaves me many a pace behind,
You roam the woodlands, far and wide,
    You quaff great draughts of country wind;
While tree and wildflower, lake and stream,
Deep shadowy nook, and sunshot gleam,
    Cool vale and far-off hill,
Each plays its mute mysterious part,
In that strange growth of mind and heart,
    I joy to witness, Will!

"Can this tall youth," I sometimes say,
    "Be mine? *my son?*" it surely seems
Scarce further backward than a day,
    Since watching o'er your feverish dreams
In that child-illness of the brain,
I thought (O Christ, with what keen pain!)
    Your pulse would soon be still,—
That all your boyish sports were o'er,
And I, heart-broken, nevermore
    Should call, or clasp you, Will!

But Heaven was kind, Death passed you by;
    And now upon your arm I lean,
My second self, of clearer eye,
    Of firmer nerve, and sturdier mien;
Through you, methinks, my long-lost youth
Revives, from whose sweet founts of truth,

And joy, I drink my fill;
I feel your every heart-throb, know
What inmost hopes within you glow,—
　　　One soul's between us, Will!

Pray Heaven that this be always so!
　　That ever on your soul and mine
Though my thin locks grow white as snow,—
　　The self-same radiant trust may shine;—
Pray that while this, my life, endures,
It aye may sympathize with yours
　　　In thought, aim, action still;
That you, O son (till comes the end),
In me may find your comrade, friend,
　　　And *more* than father, Will!

SONNET.

I CAST this sorrow from me like a crown
Of bitter nettles, and unwholesome weeds,
Nursed by cold night-dews, from malignant seeds,
Ill Fortune sowed, when all the Heaven did frown;
Its loathsome round I trample deeply down
In mire and dust, to burn my brain no more;
From off my brow I wipe the trickling gore,
While all about me, like keen clarions blown,
From breezy dells, and golden heights afar,
Their stern *reveillé* the wild March winds sound;
They wake an answering passion in my soul,
Whence, marshaled as brave warriors, taking ground
For noblest conflict, freed from doubt or dole,
Great Thoughts uprising, front Hope's morning star!

TO MY MOTHER.

LIKE streamlets to a silent sea,
   These songs with varied motion
Flow from bright Fancy's uplands free,
   To Lethe's clouded ocean;
They lapse in deepening music down
   The slopes of flower-lit meadows,
Nor dream, poor songs! how near them frown
   Oblivion's rayless shadows!

Yet though of brief and dubious life,
   All wed to incompleteness,—
The voices of these lays are rife
   With frail and fleeting sweetness;
One chord to make more full the strain,
   One note I may not smother,
Is echoed in the heart's refrain
   Which holds thy name, my mother!

To thee my earliest verse I brought,
   All wreathed in loves and roses,—
Some glowing boyish fancy, fraught
   With tender May-wind closes;
Thou did'st not taunt my fledgling song,
   Nor view its flight with scorning;
"The bird," thou said'st, "grown fleet and strong,
   Might yet outsoar the morning!"

TO MY MOTHER.

Ah me! between that hour and this,
  Eternities seem flowing;
O'er hapless graves of youth and bliss
  Dark cypress boughs are growing;
Our Fate hath dimmed with base alloy
  The rich, pure gold of pleasure,
And changed the choral chant of joy
  To Care's heart-broken measure!

But through it all,—the blight, the pall,
  The stress of thunderous weather,—
That God who keeps wild chance in thrall
  Hath linked our lots together;
So, hand in hand, we sail the gloom,
  Faith's mystic plummet casting
To sound the ways which end in bloom
  Of Edens everlasting!

I bless thee, Dear, with reverent thought!
  Pale face, and tresses hoary,
Whose every silvery thread hath caught
  Some hint of heavenly glory;—
To Thee, with trust assured, sublime,
  Death's angel-call that waitest,—
To thee, as once my earliest rhyme,
  Lo! now, I bring—my latest!

THE END.

www.ingramcontent.com/pod-product-compliance
Lightning Source LLC
Chambersburg PA
CBHW020256170426
43202CB00008B/392